P9-AOO-667

TURNAROUND: The Canadian Guide

First published in 1995 by
McGraw-Hill Ryerson Limited
300 Water Street
Whitby, Ontario
L1N 9B6

Canadian Cataloguing in Publication Data

White, Jerry, 1946-
    Turnaround: the Canadian guide
Includes bibliographical references.
ISBN 0-07-551858-9

1. Corporate turnarounds—Management. I. Shuchman, Matthew. II. Title.

HD58.8.W55 1994   658.4'063   C94-931534-6

PUBLISHER: Donald S. Broad
COVER DESIGN: Dave Hader/Studio Conceptions
EDITORIAL SERVICES: Word Guild and Marsh Hill Publishing
    Services
TEXT DESIGN AND PAGE COMPOSITION: Marsh Hill Publishing
    Services

1 2 3 4 5 6 7 8 9 0   BG   1 2 3 4 0 9 8 7 6 5

Printed and bound in Canada by Best Gagné

CONTENTS

About the Authors

Born and raised in Toronto, Jerry S. White has been a consultant, CEO and owner/manager in businesses ranging from publishing to food service. He has also been professor of management in three countries and has authored 33 books on small business, entrepreneurship, franchising, taxation, and personal finance. His syndicated column *Managing Smart* appears in 160 newspapers across North America and his radio program, *The Financial Edge,* is heard across Canada. He is also a regular contributor to *Canadian Money$aver, Canadian Living,* and *Real Estate News.* Jerry is the Chairman of J. White and Associates, Inc., merchant bankers in Toronto and New York, and he is the Personal Financial Commentator for CanWest Global TV and CFRB-1010 Radio.

Matthew L. Shuchman is a management and systems consultant based in New York and Miami. He has been a leading specialist in systems and turnaround consulting for over a decade. A former economist for the U.S. Federal Reserve, he has advised clients ranging from cruise lines and casinos to computer manufacturers and banks. His clients include Bank of Montreal, Merrill Lynch, and Soros Fund Management. He writes regularly on entrepreneurship and the management of troubled companies and is considered one of North America's leading turnaround experts.

THIS BOOK originated in our idea to write a magazine article for entrepreneurs and managers on the 101 problems faced by troubled companies trying to stay alive. We hope we have not strayed too far from our original philosophy of presenting a plain-English discussion of the major problems facing a troubled company, and offering concise solutions and examples from our own experiences and current sources.

In 1991 I moved to Florida and undertook a turnaround consulting assignment with a company that managed 17 cruise-ship-based casinos. The operations included cruises to the Caribbean, the Maritime provinces, British Columbia, Bermuda, and Alaska. The company was severely troubled, both financially and operationally. The story of this assignment truly belongs in a Travis McGee novel. I was living on board a 91-foot luxury yacht which was the sole unmortgaged asset of the company's owner. Eleven years after working as a junior economist for the U.S. Federal Reserve, I was Chief Operating Officer of the group of casinos and managing the operations of 3,000 slot machines and 200 gaming tables.

It was in Florida that I met Jerry White, who approached the company as a white knight to refinance operations. Working together on land and on sea, Jerry and I built a strong professional and personal relationship which has continued to this day. It was during one of our shipboard conversations that we both realized the great need that managers and owners of troubled companies have for common sense business advice on how to avoid failure. This book is the product of a year of writing, our interviews with managers and owners of troubled companies, and conversations with colleagues.

We have used many of our own consulting engagements as sources for the examples in the book. With a few exceptions we have tried to protect the confidentiality of those involved by disguising the identities of the individuals and the companies. Any mistakes that we have made or stories whose lessons we have misconstrued are our own failings.

Matthew L. Shuchman
September 1994
Toronto, Ontario

ACKNOWLEDGEMENTS

I would like to thank my family, most particularly my wife, Lilli, for her excellent typing and proofreading, and my son Hartley, for his computer and telecommunications assistance, which allowed me to exchange chapters with my coauthor in minutes instead of days.

J.W.
September 1994
Toronto, Ontario

First, I must acknowledge the love and support of my immediate family. My father and mother have been a source of constant encouragement, support, and welcome criticism that has extended far beyond what one should expect from parents. I am thirty-seven years old and they are still interested on a daily basis with what I am thinking, reading, and writing. My sisters Carol and Miriam (who is raising a family in Toronto) and my brother Salem have all sustained me with the emotional support that only close siblings can provide. They have all helped with their suggestions and critical comments on my experiences and writings.

Second, I must thank friends who listened to my musings that one day I would write a book about what I was doing. Many gave me examples from their own businesses and others read early drafts of the manuscript and gave helpful comments. Thank you NMB, DSS, JAR, SJB, ASM, CC, JB, PD, SK, PM, DW, JS, VSD, and BI.

Many years ago I attended Joseph Mancuso's management seminar for entrepreneurs, given under the auspices of The CEO Club, and the experience and Joe's prolific writings have had a strong effect upon my style of management.

I owe a particular debt of gratitude to my early and long-standing clients, who placed their confidence in a young entrepreneur, and from whom I learned so much more than I can say in this book by our conversations, occasional lunches, and by watching the way they managed their own firms.

Last mentioned, but foremost in my heart, I owe a debt to Lisa F. L. Waterfield. As a casino executive, not only did she teach me about her business, but she became my constant companion these past few years. Each day, Lisa would listen to the stories of my current turnaround assignment, or what I was writing about, and remind me that every reduction in personnel and every operation terminated represented names, faces, and families. She was the first to read the book and it had to pass her muster. Thank you for everything, but mostly for keeping me human.

M.L.S.
September 1994
Toronto, Ontario

To all of our friends at McGraw-Hill Ryerson, particularly our Publisher, Don Broad, thank you for your assistance in turning our manuscript into a book and for your confidence in us.

Thank you to our editor Don Loney of Word Guild and to Rachel Mansfield and Lynda Powell of Marsh Hill for their creative talents and editorial service.

We would also like to thank our U.S. publisher, AMACOM, and the American Management Association for permitting us to share our research in both the U.S. and Canada.

M.L.S. and J.W.
September 1994
Toronto, Ontario

INTRODUCTION

IN CANADA, nearly 20,000 companies will fail in 1994, a rate nearly two-and-a-half times that of the United States. 100,000 are troubled, and 250,000 are having difficulties. Signs on buildings that advertise AUCTION TODAY, GOING OUT OF BUSINESS, LOST OUR LEASE, or ONLY ~~TEN~~, ~~NINE~~, ~~EIGHT~~, SEVEN DAYS LEFT have become common scenery. Many of these impending failures can be avoided. Even in the final stages of insolvency, a turnaround is still possible.

This book teaches executives how to manage for survival and to rescue, rehabilitate, and turn around their ailing businesses. Each section teaches a practical approach for accessing one class of problems and how to solve them using real-life examples and easy-to-follow lists of what to do and what not to do.

WHO SHOULD READ THIS BOOK?

This book was written for the managers of companies who are facing difficulty or possible foreclosure, or who are asking themselves if they can afford the payroll next month. These managers are in the frontlines of a troubled company's battle for survival, and the book was written from their perspective. Using this book as a guide, many troubled companies can successfully avoid failure.

1

Anyone involved in business transactions with troubled companies will also benefit from reading this book. Those contemplating an acquisition, liquidation, or sale, court-appointed receivers and trustees, and creditors will want to read this book to learn the strategies and tactics employed by troubled companies fighting to stay alive.

More than one million North American companies deliver less-than-average performance to their owners, shareholders, and creditors. These companies are in poor health and potentially on the road to being categorized as "troubled." Investors and managers of these underperforming companies can learn valuable lessons to apply to their companies by studying their sick cousins and reading about the recommended cures for the sicknesses observed.

Even managers at healthy companies will find reading this book worthwhile by applying lessons learned from studying troubled firms to their already successful businesses.

WHAT YOU WILL LEARN BY READING THIS BOOK

After reading the book, you will understand what can be done to turn around an ailing and troubled business. You will know how to use your position as a troubled business to your advantage when negotiating, and you will learn the secret tactics others have used to stay alive. You will gain an insight into the thought processes and strategies used by failing and insolvent companies to avoid liquidation and to renegotiate liabilities, conceal and sell assets, and maintain or disguise value.

As the manager of a troubled company, you will learn how to answer critical questions including:

- Do you have enough time to turn the business around?
- What can you do to reduce costs today?
- Can part of the business be saved?
- Who are your natural allies?
- Who are your enemies?
- Can you sell the business?
- Who would be interested in buying the business?
- Will filing for bankruptcy help to achieve your goals?
- What type of bankruptcy should you consider?

• Why is returning a company to profitability easier than you expect?

Each chapter discusses the business implications of a particular problem area. Managers will learn how to solve problems using real-life examples and easy-to-follow lists of what to do and what not to do. The examples in the book are drawn from the authors' own consulting engagements and current sources.

Where bankruptcy or debtor-creditor laws may influence your company's course of actions, an overview in plain English of the legal issues is provided, along with references for further research by the reader or their attorneys. Although the book is not a replacement for good legal counsel, it will educate the business management or owners on issues to discuss with their lawyer.

How to Reduce Fixed Overhead

This book includes a step-by-step methodology with examples of how, without impairing the business, most companies can reduce their fixed-overhead costs by at least **30%**. This book teaches you how to negotiate with vendors, eliminate payables, reduce telecommunications costs, control and recover travel and entertainment expenses, and minimize insurance costs. **Thirty percenting** will be critical for all businesses competing in these difficult mid-to-late 1990s.

How to Reduce Personnel Costs

The chapter on personnel examines the hidden costs of employees and how to control and reduce the spiralling costs of providing employee benefits. The manager contemplating layoffs of employees will read about the seven alternative methods of reducing costs without the need to fire anyone. Where layoffs are necessary, the manager will learn a systematic and humane method for terminating employees.

How to Reduce Real Estate Costs

For many companies, rent or mortgage payments can be the second-largest fixed-expense category after payroll. This chapter explores methods the manager can use in reducing the costs of real estate, renegotiating lease and mortgage obligations, moving to a new location, closing unprofitable facilities, and subletting space.

How to Benefit from Media Attention

Effective public relations can be critical to a troubled firm's future success. Chapter 11 shows you how you can maintain and improve your company's public relations image, even when the business is failing, and how to use your image to help achieve your goals. Included are instructions on how to prepare and manage the publicity of adverse announcements.

How to Retain Customers and Collect Receivables

Troubled businesses often forget that their strongest supporters are their customers. In troubled times your customers can help your company to stay alive. Methods discussed in Chapter 6 include how to get your customers to take care of your payables, how to collect and verify the company's receivables, and the secrets of finding hidden value in old receivables.

How to Sell a Failing Business

You may reach the conclusion that the best course of action is to sell the company. Selling a business is the one area in which most managers have no experience. Selling a company that you are a part of is a skill that you can't learn in business school. After reading Chapter 10 you will know what to expect through the difficult emotional, legal, and business process.

This chapter covers the complete process from locating potential purchasers to preparing for the closing. Using the many examples, checklists, and how-to sections the reader learns how to write a sales memorandum; the seven places to look for potential investors; how to manage the due diligence process; and how to evaluate and negotiate with purchasers. Once you have secured a purchaser, you will learn how to move the candidate to a commitment and how to have a successful closing.

The Bankruptcy Option

Bankruptcy is discussed matter-of-factly as a business strategy. In Chapter 14 the various forms of relief available under the Bankruptcy and Insolvency Act and Company Creditors' Arrangement Act are covered including liquidations, reorganizations, and debt adjustments, with attention to both involuntary and voluntary filings.

After reading this chapter, the business owner can use bankruptcy as an effective offensive or defensive business strategy.

They will understand the relief available in bankruptcy, the impact to their business, and the pitfalls of filing without adequate preparation.

Although the book is written with a view toward managing a company to avoid bankruptcy, if your business would benefit from a bankruptcy filing or you are forced into an involuntary bankruptcy proceeding, then reading this chapter will enable you to prepare your company, your employees, and your customers to survive the bankruptcy experience.

Business bankruptcy topics covered include why most owners of small companies won't benefit from bankruptcy and the strategies for defending against an involuntary filing by creditors. Preparing for bankruptcy includes understanding these implications. Chapter 5 teaches you how to protect your business from the wrath of creditors.

The search for bankruptcy counsel is a rocky road. After reading Chapter 14, the business owner will understand who should advise them in bankruptcy and how to select a bankruptcy lawyer. Techniques covered include how to make your bankruptcy lawyer work for you and not for your creditors.

Unique to this book, because it is not written by a lawyer, are the sections on when you should not listen to your lawyer and why most bankruptcy lawyers won't tell you the truth about business failures.

The strategic objective in filing for bankruptcy is usually to safeguard the future of the owners, the business, or both, even if bankruptcy means an orderly liquidation. This chapter addresses the future implications of a bankruptcy filing to the owners, the business, and the employees.

The Importance of Security to a Troubled Company

Most firms approach security passively and react only when a problem occurs. But a troubled firm may not be able to afford even one small theft, embezzlement, or breach of security. A firm that is troubled is in greater need of security than at any other time in its history.

The discharge of employees, the closure of facilities, and the termination of operations present unique security problems. Chapter 13 addresses these problems and shows you how to safeguard proactively your company's physical assets, customer relations, and confidential information.

The reader will grasp the often neglected special security concerns of a troubled company. This chapter has many checklists and how-to sections to help the manager immediately improve the company's program.

IS YOUR COMPANY IN TROUBLE?

For some firms, the signs of impending economic distress and future financial ruin are clear. Significant litigation by customers and creditors, frozen bank accounts, Revenue Canada tax liabilities, sheriffs at the front door, and notices of eviction are obvious signs. Diminishing sales combined with shrinking bank balances and increases in payables are also indicators to more astute observers.

Some Examples of Troubled Companies

Any company that experiences declining sales for several quarters without a proportional decline in the costs of operating its business is troubled and in a nose-dive toward potential failure.

- A computer business that is too small to afford the costs of remaining on the leading edge of technology must make a decision soon or it will enter a troubled period.
- A retail clothing store with insufficient working capital to purchase inventory for the new season is facing very difficult times ahead.
- Insiders who drain a company's cash flow, beyond what it can afford, to support other ailing businesses, may be choking the only milk-bearing cow they have left.
- Companies trying to maintain an image of success above and beyond what they can afford are troubled and accelerating their impending failure.

However, not all troubled firms exhibit obvious symptoms in the early stages of their affliction. A company can have money in the bank, be current on its payments to suppliers, be making a profit, and still be "troubled." The impending loss of a major customer representing 30% of a manufacturer's revenues may not have an immediate effect on the company. The company may still show a profit for the year and have a strong balance sheet; however, the failure to replace the customer or reduce costs in short order will result in serious difficulties. This manufacturer, though not exhibiting immediate symptoms, is "troubled" and must take steps to secure its future.

How Did You Get Here?

A variety of causes can force a company into a troubled period. In the incipient stage the natural causes can include the loss of a major customer, a key employee, increased competition, loss of a major product line or vendor, failure of a planned expansion, or a simple decrease in gross profit margins. The causes can also be fraud, waste, mismanagement, poor accounting practices, theft, and embezzlement. The effect of any of these actions can cause a decrease in cash flow available to operate the business and will eventually result in serious economic troubles and the potential failure of the business.

In the next stage the company begins to exhibit the effects of decreased cash flow. These can include a reduction of assets, loss of customers, departure of employees, loss of strategic vendor relationships, and loss of prestige in the marketplace. The firm's credit becomes stretched to the limit, and creditors begin calling demanding payment. Vendors start changing payment terms from credit to COD and cash in advance. The firm may become delinquent in paying some of its fees and taxes.

Rumours begin to circulate that the company is insolvent or facing bankruptcy. Vendors send final notices, and the company rushes to make payments to avoid repossessions and terminations of essential services. Long-time customers begin to question the financial viability of the company, and vendors refuse to do business with the company unless past accounts are settled.

In the final stages, the company is usually insolvent. Litigation has been initiated by vendors and possibly customers. Legal fees become a significant part of monthly expenses. Failure to pay fees and taxes results in the assessment of penalties, and interest and charges against the company's remaining assets.

Vendors and creditors are harassing the firm daily and refuse to be put off. Management must hide to avoid unscheduled visits by creditors. Rumours of bankruptcy are widespread. The troubled company exists as a shell of its former self and is unable to grow its revenues to sustain itself.

What Can You Hope to Achieve?

If any of the characteristics of a troubled company are familiar to your company's present illness, then don't despair. Even in the final stages of insolvency, there is hope — if the business or parts of the business are **viable**.

What Are Your Goals?

Is your goal to keep the business alive and manage the transition back to profitability or to scale down, reduce costs, and try to sell the operation? Are you trying to avoid the problems resulting from personal loan guarantees? Is this a family business that you hope will provide for your children? Are you over 50 and don't know how you would make a living outside the business?

What are your goals in trying to turn around your company? Why bother? You will make more enemies than friends in trying to turn around a business. Why not just walk away and start over? Don't start the rescue mission unless you have good reasons for undertaking the assignment combined with a realistic chance of success.

Without specific, clearly defined, and — most importantly — **realistic** goals, you are running a marathon without a final destination. Knowing your goals will: (1) allow you to evaluate and select the best paths for achieving your goals, and (2) indicate to you when you have succeeded.

THE CONFLICT: WHAT IS AND WHAT COULD HAVE BEEN

As a manager or principal of a business, you may find yourself with the internal conflict between your images (read as "dreams") of how the company could be (if only you could get over this hump) and your company's present condition. When you are trying to return a company to profitability and financial stability, always strive to be a realist.

Don't abandon your dreams of what the company could be. Do, however, put them on the top shelf and concentrate your present efforts on restoring your company to a solid economic footing.

Carefully assess all of your company's assets and determine what can be achieved with your current resources. Your primary mission is to stabilize your company's present financial condition and secure its future existence or prepare to sell it for the highest offer.

Money Won't Solve Your Problems

Most troubled businesses believe that a business loan or an investment of capital will solve their problems. Although money can purchase time to solve some types of problems, in most cases money is not the underlying cause of a business's troubles and it will not secure the company's long-term future. The company may need additional funds to achieve certain goals, but capital is only **one** element of the recovery plan. Without a plan for recovery, additional funds will result only in additional debt and a further dilution of equity.

Courage Is More Important than Capital

It takes courage to write a plan for the recovery or the sale of your business. It is an admission that without the plan your business may fail. Don't forget that you are not alone in having entered a troubled period. Many of your neighbours and colleagues are in similar or worse straits.

According to Dun & Bradstreet Canada, 20,000 Canadian businesses failed in 1991, 20,000 failed in 1992, and almost 30,000 in 1993. Your advantage over these casualties is that you have recognized your difficulties and made your primary objective the charting of a course that will take you beyond the current troubled waters.

In some ways your business is unique. No other company is quite like it. However, you share many structural similarities with other businesses. Observing and analyzing the similarities found in other businesses will help you learn lessons to apply to your own company.

If you are a wholesaler, you can learn lessons from other wholesalers — both the ones that failed and those that succeeded. If you are in the service business you can learn from others in the service business, etc. A well-managed business is simply that — a well-managed business. Modelling successful practice is a useful approach.

There are many factors that contribute to the formula for success. Unfortunately, it is not always possible to determine why one company succeeds and why another company, using the same strategy, fails.

It is not usually one large error in judgement or a wrong critical decision that leads to the failure of a business. More commonly the causes of failure were several small mistakes whose consequences were ignored or overlooked by the company's management.

This book, while focusing on the strategies for recovery and resurrection, will examine the mistakes made by companies that led to their eventual failure. When managing the turnaround of a troubled company, we can learn more from observing the mistakes that other companies have made than from trying to determine the causes of their successes.

Using this book as a guide, you can successfully avoid failure.

CHAPTER I

MANAGING
UNDER
FIRE

OUR ORIGINAL GOAL was to write a book about business pathology, analyzing why a business fails and what managers and owners could do about it. The number of Canadian business failures quadrupled from 1979 to 1985 and net new business formation declined by 24% in the same period. Needless to say, because the country did not learn from the period's results, the rate of failure was replicated again from 1988 to 1993.

Dun & Bradstreet's analysis of business failure in Canada from 1980-1990 shows that 67% of business failures are caused by various management shortcomings. These range from the lack of planning and controls to excess overheads and new product launch failure. Only 3% to 5% are caused by fraud, 5% to 10% by adverse economic conditions, and 5% by the inability to obtain new financing.

BUSINESS PATHOLOGY

We decided that a theory of business pathology — we entitled it "The Art of Management Failure" — would not be the positive motivating text or panacea that management would be looking for. Therefore, to avoid our own failure we decided to look at the results of this mismanagement and produce a set of meaningful actions to save business from failure.

No Glory in Failure

There is no glamour or glory in failure. There will be no magazine covers extolling your brilliance, no prizes for quality, no after-dinner speeches at the Jaycees. Yet we can learn a lot from studying and analyzing failure. As in any pathology, it shows us what causes death and what to avoid. But North American managers want solutions with catchy phrases that are simple, fast, and cheap.

The failure industry — corporate turnaround specialists — is relatively new and uninfluential. Few professionals want to be associated with failures and losers, and the pain and suffering of workouts, turnarounds, and retrenchments.

Dayton Ogden, CEO of one of North America's premier executive search firms, SpenserStuart, speaks of the lack of leadership talent to handle the challenges of the mid-'90s economy. We need people who can do more with less, communicate well, and make a profit. Most of his searches in 1993-94 were for CEOs to take charge of troubled companies including IBM and Canadian Tire.

Failure as a Right

Companies in distress are highly pervasive. While about 56% of firms manage to survive their first eight years according to a study of 810,000 North American businesses by the New Jersey Institute of Technology, 44% do not. Less than half of the 1970 Fortune 500 are still around, and only 300 of the 1994 Fortune 500 will be around in the year 2000.

Failure is everywhere — as it should be in a free economy. One of the great rights of a free economy is the right to fail. After all, is it not the purpose of competition and competitive strategy to eliminate the competition and eventually to get a 100% monopoly, or at least a psychological monopoly in the customers' minds that only you can satisfy their needs with your products, services, or retail environment?

No Theory of Turnarounds

Any review of the literature in this field shows that there is no unifying theory of turnarounds, no common taxonomy or classification system or even a universally accepted lexicon of terms.

One of the authors, a professor of management at three different graduate business schools in three countries, found that the concept of saving a business or even considering failure is rarely taught.

Yes, there are cases taught of businesses with a badly launched product or poor distribution, but few business schools believe failure or its long-term solution is worthy of study.

For the last 30 years, growth and strategy formation have been the focus of manufacturing firms with strong or potential competitive advantage. The firm is always dealing from strengths, with substantial resources, and not from a need to survive or turn itself around.

Innumerable books have been written on the subjects of growth, mergers, and vertical integration, but not on dismemberment or business resurrection.

BUSINESS HAS CHANGED

In the low growth, low inflation 1990s, things have changed. Nearly 80% of all businesses are in retailing and services. Business is global. Financing for small and medium-sized business is hard to come by despite record 20-year-low interest rates.

Management experts now write of the failure of business schools to teach such relevant skills as leadership, communication, and entrepreneurship. The concept of teaching restructuring and downsizing was not necessary if there was unlimited growth. The conclusion appears to be that the preoccupation with growth is widely reported as the primary cause of corporate financial decline.

By 1990, economists were saying we were "overstored," "overmalled," and "overfactoried." For the first time since the Second World War we have excess market supply over demand. About 2,700,000 white-collar managers have lost their jobs. Most are over 40 with little likelihood of direct corporate reemployment. Office vacancies average nearly 17% across the United States, industrial space vacancies sit at nearly 20%. There has been real price deflation in many product categories and increasing prices to get a better cash flow from the business may no longer be an option. Growth in market share growth is not possible in many business categories with an older, more conservative customer base. Generation "X" is not optimistic about the next decade and the "Yuppies" are now "Dumpies."

SURVIVAL AND RESURRECTION

Retrenchment is defined as the significant reduction of costs, assets, product lines, retail locations, employers, and overheads. This book is not just about the process of retrenchment, but about the concepts of turnaround—**survival and resurrection.**

Retrenchment is a component of the turnaround process—in a way an operational reaction or response to financial decline and the failure of business strategy. The goal is the strategic generation of cash flow to bring the firm back to profitability and to focus on the business segments with the best probability of survival and profit growth.

We have long been advocates of "logical incrementalism" instead of long-term strategic planning. Logical incrementalism requires us to learn from experiences and continuously and gradually change our strategies over time to avoid failure. But once in difficulty, being patient or trying to muddle through may not be enough.

New strategies alone cannot alter the consequences of a hostile economic or competitive environment or the failure of management to perform effectively.

We disagree in part with John Goldhammer in his otherwise excellent book, *The Save Your Business Book* when he suggests, "No business difficulty is permanent. It will pass."[1] It will only pass when it is made to, by recognition and action.

Most attempts to save a severely troubled business do not succeed. Only about 10% of firms survive the Company Creditors' Arrangement Act and come out alive, because they don't understand how to utilize the reorganization process strategically.

As Richard Sloma suggests in his classic *The Turnaround Managers Handbook,* "Turnarounds also fail because they are initiated and implemented in the same manner and by the same people who allowed the firm to get into trouble in the first place."[2] We believe there is a process and methodology for the logical salvation of the business and procedures for its eventual resurrection.

In the *Turnaround Survival Guide,* David Silver agrees that "there is a process for saving the troubled company just as there is a process for starting a company, or expanding a company, for buying a company, or selling a company."[3]

Mark Goldston, now famous for his revival of LA Gear, suggests in *The Turnaround Prescription,* "Businesses do not decline on their own; they are managed into and through the process."[4]

To understand the concept of the *Turnaround* and how to manage under fire, you must first understand what businesses qualify for the turnaround process, the severity of the problem, the difference between long- and short-term solutions and the types of internal and external problems a business can face. *Turnaround: The Canadian Guide* is about the process and procedures of turnaround survival and resurrection.

Turnaround = Forced Change

Retrenchment is a competitive action that can reverse the impact of poor management. It is a basic strategy for firms that face eroding markets and declining profit margins. The process of retrenchment for the business is usually an essential element prior to implementing a new action plan.

A company in need of being "Managed Under Fire" can be characterized as one that has

- been operating under a poor and ineffective strategy
- suffered from the poor implementation of an otherwise good strategy
- experienced poor operations represented by lost sales from bad service, high costs, and poor product reliability
- experienced poor operational efficiency through high overheads, poor turnaround, and high inventory costs.

Are you in need of a turnaround? A turnaround situation exists for any firm that on an industry or sector specific basis

- has two or more years of substandard ROI
- has three or more years of sub-GNP growth in income
- has two or more years of 10% or more decline in net profit
- has performance in earnings consistently below the industry standard and regularly below 10%.

The process of responding to the various problems of Managing Under Fire toward Forced Change is affected by both the severity of the decline faced by the firm and whether the factors causing the problems are internal or external.

Severity

Problems that are not severe are normally responded to by cutbacks and overall cost reductions. Severe problems are responded to by drastic cost reductions as well as asset reductions and dispositions. This condition, called **situation severity**, is represented by sales and margin declines in cases of mild severity to imminent bankruptcy in situations of extreme severity.

Life Cycle

The market or company life cycle is also a factor. Firms in weak market positions in growing markets can succeed by cutting back and restructuring. Firms in mature or declining sectors must focus on efficiency of operations to provide the low costs needed in order to survive.

Causality

Causality is a prime determinant of response strategy. If the problems are internal to the business, then solutions tend to be focused on efficiency and management styles, while externally caused problems are responded to by entrepreneurial-driven reconfiguration of the remaining business assets. This means doing things differently than in the past and can include strategies such as

- lower prices
- new product launchings
- repositioning and relaunching older products
- redesigning and repositioning stores
- adding new services with a larger "bundle of benefits"
- renewing advertising with a stronger sales effort.

If you are under the pressure of forced change, you must ensure that the entity survives in some fashion, then is resurrected and relaunched as an essentially "new" and improved venture.

THE INTERACTION FACTOR

Once the problems have been identified, we have seen and successfully implemented many resurrection strategies over the years. We recognize the interrelationship of all of these seven strategic elements. When we change a business strategy, we also need to consider its structure, systems, staff, skills, management styles, and superordinate goals (culture). These factors change whether we like it or not and are inseparable. Therefore, to ensure effective transformational results we must consider them all.

The four most often mentioned approaches to forced change are:

1. Cutbacks — cutting costs, new financial and expense controls and disposing of losing lines, subsidiaries or stores;
2. Restructuring — organizational structural change and new methods;
3. Management — new CEOs, new business mission statements, new leadership team;
4. Growth — new promotional methods, acquisitions, new markets, new product lines or stores.

A total approach appropriate to the business situation, the severity of the problem, and its causes is needed. Even the above four mentioned methods are interrelated and should be considered in their totality and synergy.

EXHIBIT 1-1

RESPONSES TO BUSINESS PROBLEMS WHEN MANAGING UNDER FIRE

SITUATIONAL SEVERITY

Mild

Cutbacks

Cost Cutting

Operational Efficiency

Entrepreneurial Reconfiguration

Revenue Generation

Growth

External Cause

Internal Cause

Management Styles

Asset Sales

Focus on Highest Profit Potential Components of the Business

Business Sale

Bankruptcy and Insolvency Act

Company Creditors' Arrangement Act

Severe

NOTES

[1]*The Save Your Business Book: A Survival Manual for Small Business Owners*, John Goldhammer. New York: Lexington Books, 1993, p. 4.

[2]*The Turnaround Managers Handbook*, Richard Sloma. New York: Free Press, 1988, p. 22.

[3]*The Turnaround Survival Guide: Strategies for the Company in Crisis*, A. David Silver. Chicago: Dearborn Financial Publishing, Inc., 1992, p. 2.

[4]*The Turnaround Prescription: Repositioning Troubled Companies*, Mark R. Goldston. New York: Free Press, 1992, p. 34.

CHAPTER 2

SURVIVAL
AND
RESURRECTION
PLANNING

LEE IACCOCA understood what to do when he stepped into the troubled Chrysler Corporation. He recognized that with a 2,100,000 car-a-year breakeven point, he could not survive. Chrysler had to become a low-cost producer, close all unprofitable and antiquated operations, reestablish a market position based on product innovation, and reschedule and restructure its debt.

Iaccoca established a two-part process: first survival. He cut his breakeven point to 1,000,000 cars a year and forced creditors to reschedule his debt. Then resurrection — the "K" car followed by the Minivan and Jeep.

The demise in Canada since 1990 of over 400 retail chains, Olympia & York, and more than 2,000 small manufacturers, is a sad tale of excess leverage, overbuilt markets, poor management and the classic stage of businesses failing to evolve and change over time.

Canadians in many areas opposed the North American Free Trade Agreement and the elimination of tariffs — they could hide behind barriers and not have to compete with innovation and aggression.

The failure rate of Canadian businesses is two-and-a-half times the U.S. rate for a reason. Businesses fight for a smaller market, earn lower margins, have higher costs and more expensive financing. In light of this, Canadians must be more creative and work harder to survive, especially in difficult times.

Every successful manager in a turnaround recognizes that a two-step plan is needed in a severe situation. The first part is the survival plan, the second the resurrection plan.

THE SURVIVAL AND RESURRECTION PLANNING PROCESS

Once you begin "The Turnaround," a planning process is needed. If you are an outsider brought in to effect the turnaround, you will have about a week to get organized and about three weeks to put the plan together.

Existing management will have less time. You will be the subject of scrutiny and calls to find out what you plan to do. Hasty action provoked by the need to be seen to be doing something could be fatal. What counts is that we have a logical plan in place that recognizes the problems, their source, and severity, and that there are specific action plans in place to effect change.

At the end of each action plan, you will need to know who will do what, by when, and with what intended result. This type of action accountability will be essential to the success of this plan.

Measurement and evaluation in a troubled business must be done on a dynamic basis. Either we have the cash to pay our bills or we go out of business. What are the cash consequences of all actions and transactions? Where are we at the end of each day and each week? Cash flow statements become our strategic survival guides.

The moment the decision is made to produce the plan a team must be established to assemble the information, create the action plans, and formulate implementation and evaluation processes. This team will be responsible for the plan's success.

This is not a five-year strategic plan which rarely works. It is a one-month/six-month/one-year program for survival and a six-month/one-year/two-year plan to follow for resurrection. While the resurrection plan may be run concurrently if the cash flow and resources are present, there is usually a delay or time lag of three to six months before a resurrection plan begins its parallel progress.

Choosing the Turnaround Team

Returning the troubled company to profitability will usually involve terminations of operations and personnel. You cannot openly discuss these types of decisions with all of your employees. Choose your team wisely. Select as team members only the managers you need and those you can trust.

For the most part, you should ignore company politics in making your selections. If the company is forced to close its doors, then politics won't matter. When managing the turnaround, you are unlikely to make any new friends, so don't try and appease individuals whose termination you may be forced to recommend tomorrow.

Candidates for the turnaround team should be independent thinkers, entrepreneurial, professionally capable, flexible in playing more than one role, and effective at playing on a team with managers who hold opposing viewpoints.

The successful turnaround team has a flat hierarchy with one leader who is supported by a group of implementors. Each implementor is responsible for a discrete area, but they should all feel comfortable working with team members on areas outside of their direct control.

THE SURVIVAL RETREAT

With limited resources and a need to be on site to cope with fires the management group will have to get the job done in no more than three days of uninterrupted work. This means that careful front-end work is needed in gathering information and in structuring the time available — 36 to 40 hours.

The optimal locations are away from the business. A nearby hotel or someone's recreation room is superior to the boardroom or office. Meals can be brought in and participants can stay overnight at the hotel. After three days of living in very close quarters, everyone is highly motivated to get the job done.

With large corporations we usually had the breathing space and time of at least a month. We started in the office for a week gathering files, followed by a weekend retreat at a hotel, then back to the office for two weeks then to the hotel for a further Friday to Monday final session.

The survival plan that resulted was implemented while we worked on resurrection that included possible sale, mergers, and divestiture of assets. This usually took another 90 days before it could be implemented.

THE INFORMATION YOU WILL NEED

Give assignments to each of the team to bring the information needed for the discussions. Tell each participant precisely what information they are responsible for and the amount of detail required. Put all information requests in writing and be explicit about the period and detail required.

Don't assume in your requests for information that someone will know "what you mean." Most employees have little or no background in statistics and will generate reports describing changes of .01% when the accuracy of the underlying information is + or − 1%. If you want figures rounded to the nearest dollar, or nearest thousand dollars, then say so.

The Importance of Verification

Be certain that your instructions include a request for the manager to verify personally the accuracy of the reports. Often we have observed blatant errors in financial reports, reprinted for months and sometimes for years, because of a lack of designated accountability for the contents of the report.

Throughout this book you will read repeated warnings that information which has not been verified is useless in the decision making process. Believe it!

The company you are trying to return to good health did not become ill because of false or misleading information, but without **accurate** information you will be unable to make the informed decisions that are both necessary and essential to turning your company around.

Some information you need may already be available in your company's files. However, unless you are willing to verify the accuracy of the information, you are foolish to use it. Rely upon reports only after you have verified the accuracy of the information they contain.

Accurate information is critical to the survival and resurrection plan. Without it you are doomed to failure. If you are an outsider, brought in as a new saviour, be wary of what you receive and verify it for content and source.

Are Certified Audits Useful?

Even information certified by public accounting firms should be viewed with suspicion. In several recent bankruptcy cases, charges of fraud and negligence have been brought against their auditors by trustees, shareholders, and creditors after discovering "irregularities" in the historical financials of the bankrupt companies. Most of these cases have been settled out of court, but the size and frequency of these settlements are very disturbing to investors and creditors, who rely upon "certified" audits for making business decisions to extend credit and make investments.

W A R N I N G

Managers of troubled companies should be cautious about using any financial reports generated without their personal supervision.

Principal Group of Alberta, famous for its bankruptcy and liquidation that cost western Canadians tens of millions of dollars, was regularly audited by its accountants and provincial regulators. Its business practices seemed to escape the process. The resultant collapse affected thousands and the auditors settled out of court.

Canadian banks are inspected by both internal auditors and shareholders' outside auditors each year. Each branch is individually inspected. Yet in northern Ontario, an employee of a major bank embezzled over $500,000 over a period of years and survived three complete audits.

WHAT CAN WE CONCLUDE ABOUT REPORTS BY CA FIRMS?

Unfortunately, an audit is only as good as the information upon which it is based, and unscrupulous corporate officers or persons in positions of trust, can become very adept at methods of concealing fraud from auditors.

Professor Roman L. Weil of the University of Chicago's Graduate School of Business, who teaches auditing, places the blame on the auditor's training. Weil states, "The auditor does have an obligation to keep its eyes open, but it starts out with the assumption that management is honest. So if management sets out to systematically fool the auditor, they are going to fool the auditor."

The late Ralph Fisher, one of Canada's founding forensic accountants, in 1989 advised, "Most auditors couldn't see a fraud if they fell over it. We just don't teach them to be suspicious or aggressive in their quest."[1]

Although Mr. Fisher's judgement may be too harsh, the recent surge of fraud committed by insiders who successfully pulled the wool over the eyes of trained groups of auditors certainly says that auditors need to look closer and dig deeper.

In most of the previously mentioned cases of fraud, the procedures that were followed were not different from those used at hundreds of firms where no fraud existed.

Sources in the accounting trade, although not defending their colleagues who were negligent in failing to detect irregularities, say that to verify all of the numbers that are required for a certified audit would raise professional fees to levels that many companies would be unwilling to pay.

The conclusion to be drawn by the manager of a troubled business is that all reports based on information generated without proper supervision, or where the numbers were not externally verified, must be treated with suspicion.

In a turnaround situation, there is very little room for mistakes in valuing assets and liabilities and calculating the financial health of the subject company. All information collected prior to the initiation of the project should be regarded with suspicion until proven accurate.

DOCUMENTS FOR SURVIVAL PLANNING

Exhibit 2-1 is a comprehensive list of the information that is recommended (i.e., desirable) for a first survival meeting. The documents are divided into groups by the department that should be responsible for the information. If some of the information is unavailable, don't delay — hold the meeting anyway.

Reports from the Accounting Department

The accounting department is an important source for the compilation of reports necessary for making strategic decisions. Unfortunately, this department is also usually staffed by the lowest-paid (and often the most overworked) clerical employees in the company.

EXHIBIT 2-1

RECOMMENDED DOCUMENTS FOR SURVIVAL PLANNING		
ORIGIN	DESCRIPTION	PERIOD
Accounting	Balance sheet (quarterly)	Last 4 quarters
	List of all business liabilities	Current
	List of all business assets	Current
	Income statement (monthly)	Last 12 months
	Cash flows (quarterly)	Last 4 quarters
	Cash flow projections (weekly)	Next 12 weeks
	Summary of outstanding taxes	Current
	Projection of outstanding taxes	Next 6 months
Personnel	All wages, salaries, and commissions	Current & due
	Organizational chart of the company	Current
	Company's personnel policy book	Current
Purchasing	List of suppliers and vendors	Current
	List of accounts payable (AP)	Current
	List of disputed AP	Last 2 years
Sales	List of customers	Current
	List of accounts receivable (AR)	Current
	List of uncollectible AR	Last 2 years
Executive	List of competitors & future partners	Current
Legal	Summary of outstanding litigation	Current
Warehouse	Inventory list	Current

Although the balance sheet should encompass a list of all business liabilities and assets, request a separate list of these items to corroborate the balance sheet and to identify areas for future investigation. Not all assets and liabilities appear on the balance sheet. This is either because they cannot be properly categorized or, in the case of related entities, the item needs to appear on the balance sheet of more than one company.

Business liabilities should include all accounts payable (AP), and all scheduled debts such as loans, mortgages, leases, credit card payments, and utilities. Assets of the business should include all bank accounts, stocks and investments, real estate, vehicles, major equipment, insurance claims due, accounts receivable (AR), deposits, and refunds due.

Both the lists of business liabilities and assets should be ranked in descending order and annotated with sufficient description that further investigation is possible without the need to consult the report's author.

The most important reports that the accounting department is responsible for are the cash flow projections. These reports should be done with the inclusion of the most conservative estimate of potential future income and with the most liberal estimate of future expenses.

Ask for these reports as soon as you realize the company is in trouble. Don't waste time waiting for computer programming to generate these reports. Cash flow projections can be easily constructed by hand or using a personal computer and a spreadsheet package.

The summary of outstanding taxes should be divided into two categories: corporate liabilities and tax and vacation pay obligations.

Tax and vacation funds are those taxes that the company collects as the agent of a governmental taxing authority or as a statutory obligation. They are the most urgent taxes to pay because the directors and principals — and even the managers of the company — can be held personally liable, and the liability is usually not dischargeable in bankruptcy. Included in this list of taxes are sales taxes, GST, payroll withholding taxes, Canada Pension, unemployment insurance, and workers' compensation.

Many taxes collected become liabilities when the transaction being taxed takes place (i.e., payroll is earned or sale occurs) but are not "due" (i.e., paid to the government) until the end of the month or quarter. To encompass these potential obligations, you should request a list of all "new" taxes that are estimated as becoming due over the next six months.

Reports from the Personnel Department

The report of all wages, salaries, and commissions (see Exhibit 2-2) is one of the essential elements in examining the costs savings that could be realized in terminating or reducing operations. The report should include the full monthly cost of each employee or regular consultant and independent contractor.

In addition to salary and taxes, full cost includes any regularly paid benefits such as life and health insurance, car allowances, housing allowances, educational benefits, and commissions. The report is most useful if ranked in order of descending total compensation.

EXHIBIT 2-2

ALL WAGES, SALARIES, AND COMMISSIONS REPORT						
NAME	MONTHLY GROSS SALARY	HEALTH AND LIFE INSURANCE	AUTO AND OTHER BENEFITS	TAXES, CPP, UIC, WC*	TOTAL MONTHLY COST	% SHARE
Jose	4,000	400	500	600	5,500	31.5
Lawrence	2,000	200	0	300	2,500	14.0
Ranjit	3,000	300	200	450	3,950	22.5
Tom the Consultant	2,500	0	0	0	2,500	14.0
Mindel	1,500	150	0	225	1,875	11.0
Wanchu	1,000	100	0	150	1,250	7.0
Totals	14,000	1,150	700	2,100	17,575	100.0
% share	78	6	4	12		

*Taxes include Canada Pension, Unemployment Insurance, and Workers' Compensation.

Although organizational charts generated by the personnel department may be of limited usefulness, they provide a starting point for the team to work with.

The company's personnel policy book is important because it states the company's policy on retirement, termination, and severance. The team will need this information when estimating the cost of terminating or reducing operations. If the company doesn't have a written policy on personnel, then the limitations are those imposed by certain federal and provincial authorities in terms of payoffs and notice periods. These are usually dependent on business size and whether it is federally regulated, such as an airline, or comes under provincial labour codes.

Reports from the Purchasing Department

The list of major suppliers and vendors should include a brief description of each supplier including products or services purchased, payment terms, amounts past due, and disputes about shipments. The report should also include at least one alternate supplier for each major purchasing category.

Though the list of accounts payable would normally come from the accounting department, without the annotations of those responsible for purchasing, the report lacks the required detail. Ask the purchasing department to annotate both the current AP list and the list of disputed accounts payable. Both lists should be ranked in descending order of the outstanding balances, along with aging for each account.

Reports from the Sales Department

The sales department should provide a complete list of all customers who have done business with the company during the past year and should obtain a copy of the accounts receivable (AR) reports from the accounting departments and annotate it as required.

Where an account is listed as uncollectible or disputed, the sales department should be required to provide additional information as to the circumstances surrounding the problem and any potential resolution. Specify that you want to know about any inventory that is at a customer's site on a provisional, loan, or trial basis. All lists should be ranked in descending order of the outstanding balances along with aging information for each account.

Report from the Executive Branch

The lists of competitors and future potential partners will be required to explore candidates for sales of inventory, outplacement of employees, and potential investors in your company. Included in your list of current competitors should be both your friends and your adversaries. As long as the price is right, why should you care if the purchaser was formerly a bitter enemy. The list of potential partners should include related businesses and firms in the same business in different geographical and discrete markets.

Report from the Legal Department

Either your inside legal counsel or the person responsible for managing the company's outside counsel should write a brief summary of all outstanding litigation, arbitration, judgements, and proceedings in which the company or its principals are involved.

Report from the Warehouse

Although the accounting department should have a list of the company's inventory, we rarely trust these reports. The staff of the warehouse is usually more knowledgeable than management as to the quantities and condition of goods in the warehouse. Choose a trusted manager to oversee a spot inventory of all goods in the warehouse and in other storage facilities.

This basic collection of information is the core of the survival plan. It will help us cut our costs and improve survival cash. The turnaround team should be able to formulate plans based on the detailed analysis for each business segment we provide later in the book.

RESURRECTION PLANNING

Once the business survival plan has been established, we can then proceed to think on a long-term basis. The basic fire is out. Now is the time for entrepreneurial change, asset disposition, strategic partnerships, and repositioning of the business long term — the next six months to two years.

In later chapters we will deal in greater detail with asset disposition as well as the sale of the business.

The basic planning model and process is not unlike what we did for survival. We gather facts, prepare for a retreat, assemble the team, analyze the information, and prepare an action plan with specific responsibilities and time frames.

Documents Needed for Resurrection Planning

- Previous year's strategic plans and budgets
- List of all stores, offices, warehouses, locations
- List of leases
- Detailed competitors list with evaluation of strengths and weaknesses
- Marketing plans

- List of all products, costs, product lines sold, institutional agreements
- All advertising and promotion copy
- List of major customers and suppliers
- Any current consumer or market research
- List of key personnel
- Industry or sector data on growth, trends.

Analyzing the Business

There are many ways to examine the business. Divide the company into operational areas and then draw a functional segmentation diagram. Using the segmentation, it's a straightforward process to take the information from the financial reports and perform a preliminary analysis of the profitability of each segment. Using profitability as a guide you can begin making decisions on which areas to concentrate your efforts.

To analyze the profitability of each segment, you will need to determine which segments are responsible for expenses and which are responsible for revenue. Although at first glance it would appear that most businesses should already know where their revenue comes from, our experience has shown otherwise.

An early rule to follow in managing a troubled company is to discard your first assumptions. Most companies know where their gross revenues come from but are not infrequently mistaken about the net profit derived from each segment or division.

Segregate the business into distinct and functional areas. The firm may already be divided into different departments, groups, or products, depending on your type of business. In constructing a model of your company the differentiation by function is the most important (i.e., at the top level of the hierarchy).

Building a Functional Model of Your Business

All businesses, even those with only one employee, have different functional areas. Each employee in a small business may wear more than one hat (i.e., perform more than one function) and in a large company, more than one person may wear the same hat. Both large and small companies can be divided into functional operational areas.

Exhibit 2-3 shows examples of several businesses that have been divided into functional areas. We will call this mode of analysis the "functional segmentation" of a business. The examples are a service business (which could be a carpet cleaning business, or a professional firm such as a medical, legal, or accounting practice) and a product distribution firm. Exhibit 2-4 expands upon the functional segmentation of the product distribution company.

EXHIBIT 2-3

EXAMPLES OF FUNCTIONAL SEGMENTATION				
SERVICE BUSINESS				
Producers		Sales		Administration
PRODUCT DISTRIBUTION FIRM				
Purchasing	Sales	Service	Accounting	Warehouse

EXHIBIT 2-4

EXPANDING UPON THE FUNCTIONAL SEGMENTATION			
PRODUCT DISTRIBUTION FIRM			
PURCHASING			
New products	Major products		Parts and supplies
SALES			
Inside	Foreign sales	Major account	Outside
SERVICE			
Inside	Outside		Inside
ACCOUNTING			
Accounts receivable	Accounts payable	Payroll & Personnel	General ledger & Taxes
WAREHOUSE			
Used equipment	New equipment		Supplies

In this example, purchasing is the primary category under which three types of purchases are made: new products, existing major product lines, and purchases of service parts and supplies for the company. The functions of the sales, service, accounting, and warehouse departments have also been treated in the same way.

Profit Contribution Analysis of Each Segment

The next step is to examine the operations of the firm and directly allocate for the past year (or at the least, the most recent six-month period) the revenues received and expenses incurred by each functional area (segment). Use the financial documentation that you prepared for the meeting as the source.

Allocating Expenses

For some categories of expenses, such as the payroll cost of a salesperson, allocating the expense to one category is a simple task.

For other categories, such as the cost of the company van (used by the purchasing, service, and warehouse departments), attributing the cost to one department is not possible. Where it is not possible to allocate the entire expense item to a specific operation at the second level, then allocate it to a primary function and you can apportion it later.

Some expenses such as utility costs (telephone, electricity, water, gas, etc.) will be difficult to allocate even at the primary level, so attribute these costs to general overhead. Later, you can apportion these general overhead costs into pro-rated portions for the primary and secondary levels.

Allocating Revenues

Perform the same exercise as you did for dividing expenses to attributing the revenues for your firm. Don't worry that your service department has no revenue and only expenses. You can insist that without a service department you wouldn't have any sales, but the purpose of the exercise is not to decide which departments to eliminate, but rather to target those areas that require attention first.

Allocating General Overhead

When it is difficult to allocate the full amount of the revenue or expense to one functional segment, use another expense or revenue category as a guide to how to divide it between more than one segment. For example, you may find it difficult to divide the utility costs between the accounting and the purchasing departments. However, you know that purchasing occupies only 1,000 sq. ft. of a 10,000 sq. ft. office building and accounting occupies approximately 3,000 sq. ft. To apportion utility costs, attribute 10% of the utility bill to purchasing and 30% to accounting.

Turnaround Team Discussion

Gather the turnaround team together and discuss the results of your analysis. Your aim is to direct discussion toward two important issues: (1) What business are we in? and (2) What business do we want to be in?

What Business Are We In?

There is more than one way to answer this question. One approach is to assess where the company's efforts are devoted, where

EFFORTS = CAPITAL + LABOUR + MANAGEMENT ATTENTION.

An automobile dealership that devotes 75% of its overhead and most of its management attention to a truck sales division that generates only losses may view itself as being in the business of selling trucks, even though it derives its profits elsewhere.

Another approach, preferred in the turnaround scenario, is to examine the net revenue attributed to each functional area and rank the areas in order of descending revenues.

You may believe that you are in the business of **selling** new lawn mowers until you discover that more than half your net revenues derived from your **service** of used mowers, not sales of new mowers.

What Business Do We Want To Be In?

Now consider the question: "What business do we want to be in?" One choice is the business that is best for you on a personal basis, and another is the business that is best to be in during this recovery period. Finally, there is the choice of what business you desire to be in for the future.

Is each department profitable? A response that the service department is unprofitable but without it you couldn't sell new equipment is improper at this juncture. If someone were to tell you that you could only operate one department, and your objective was to retain the most profitable area, what would you keep?

Considering the Company's Options

With improved cash flow and some financial stability, the company can now consider more options and alternatives. The planning process will identify the optimal routes to follow. These may include many repositioning strategies plus the eventual sale of the business or its component parts. During the option-generation process you can assess new directions for the business, whether new management staff are needed, and whether you believe the business is viable in the long term.

20 RULES TO REMEMBER WHEN MANAGING UNDER FIRE

1. Your first assumptions are usually correct.
2. Support management decisions by collection of data and analysis, not by relying on old maxims.
3. Don't rely upon information that cannot be verified.
4. Never minimize the magnitude of an expense or the benefits of a cost reduction without measuring it.
5. There are no "fixed" expenses. "Fixed" only means you can quantify the expense before renegotiating it.
6. If maxims are used around your company to explain or justify decisions, be certain that these maxims are representative of your corporate image and philosophy.
7. The cardinal rule of the troubled firm when negotiating is: *if those you do business with will benefit more by your staying in business than by your closing, then you have leverage and should use it.*
8. Even when managing under fire, the standard rules of good management still apply.
9. Don't model management's behaviour upon Arnold Schwarzenegger's portrayal of a futuristic hit man in *The Terminator.* Don't try to imitate Jimmy Stewart in *It's a Wonderful Life,* either.
10. A good manager should be effective, efficient, and compassionate, yet remain firm when executing decisions.
11. Only children like surprises; nobody in business likes surprises.
12. Your current counsel (accountants, lawyers, and consultants) are probably not qualified to give you advice when you are facing economic failure or insolvency.

13. Use professionals only for their specialty.
14. Be ever vigilant for, and conscious of, conflicts of interest.
15. Confirm all "understandings" in writing.
16. You have no true friends in business. Your "friends" are primarily in business to make a profit; friendship is secondary.
17. The best forms of payment are cash, cashier's cheque, or certified cheque, in that order.
18. Look to see if cost centres can be made into profit centres.
19. The 30% rule applies to nearly all business. All costs, when reduced by "Thirty Percenting," yield survival numbers.
20. First, you must assure your survival; second, you work on the plan for resurrection.

NOTES

[1]*The Plain Dealer*, April 4, 1993.

CHAPTER 3

REDUCING OVERHEAD

To REDUCE EXPENSES the best advice is *stop spending money!*

Cash is king and right now your company needs every bit of cash to survive. Reducing expenses is not a project for one day, it's a philosophy of business. We agree with management guru Peter Drucker who says, "Absorption of overhead is one of the most obscene terms I have ever heard."

Do not permit yourself to speak in terms of an Accounting 101 phrase like... the **amount** of overhead that can be supported by the current business...

The only "amount of overhead" that a company should "support" are those expenses that are **absolutely** necessary for the business to be profitable.

Any other expenses are luxuries and fringe benefits. For tax purposes we may call these extraneous expenses "overhead" but we all know they are luxuries and unnecessary.

MANAGING FOR SURVIVAL vs. MANAGING FOR SUCCESS

Before your company became immersed in troubled waters you were managing for success and your objective was to maximize the long-term prosperity of the business.

Now you are managing for survival and your objective is to keep the company's head above water and chart a course that will stabilize the company's future financial position.

You are not "down-sizing" your company, but in the terminology of the '90s, you are "right-sizing" your company. The business should never have become encumbered by expenses that are unnecessary to make a profit.

While trying to "right-size" your company, you may not actually reduce true "overhead." You can, however, reduce the list of expenses that are treated as overhead and then eliminate or curtail these unnecessary expenses.

WHAT DO YOU REALLY NEED TO SURVIVE?

As the manager of a troubled company, the questions you must ask every day are, "What does the business really need to survive?" and "How can I stretch my cash flow to get the production out the door?" With this in mind, examine the regular expenses that your company incurs and determine if anything can be done to reduce them.

As a senior manager, you are unlikely to know all of the areas where waste occurs. Your junior managers and the troops, however, will always know where the excesses are. You don't need to teach your employees how to reduce costs — they already know how. What you must inspire in each is the philosophy that reducing costs is necessary for the company to remain competitive, stay in business, and protect their jobs.

Senior management must set an example. Don't be a skinflint, but try to set the example that everyone can economize. Driving a new Mercedes to work and then lecturing managers on the urgent need to reduce costs isn't likely to be very effective.

> In a turnaround, there are no "fixed" expenses. "Fixed" only means you can quantify the expense before re-evaluating your needs or renegotiating the costs.

The list of expenses that should be examined for possible reduction or elimination is different for each type of business. The following list details a few general areas where cost savings can be found.

EXPENSES TO REDUCE OR ELIMINATE		
Airline tickets	Maintenance contracts	Subscriptions
Auto rentals	Office supplies	Taxicab costs
Beverage costs	Overnight couriers	Telephone costs
Company food	Packing materials	Transportation costs
Education costs	Parts	Travel
Hotel costs	Photocopying	Utility costs
HVAC costs	Postage	Vacation days
Landscaping	Shipping	Vehicle maintenance
Laundry	Sick days	Waste removal

THIRTY PERCENTING

Although each troubled company is different, by carefully examining all areas of the company's operations most managers will discover that savings of 30% of expenses are realizable. Some turnaround experts will tell you to cut expenses until it hurts, then cut some more. Readers of this chapter will learn many ways to reduce expenses without the pain. By instilling a philosophy of conservation and managing for survival, 30% reductions in the level of expenses can be achieved without inflicting trauma upon the surviving employees.

Making Managers Accountable for Expenses

One way to start the process of cost reduction is to make each manager responsible for, and **accountable for**, the expenses of their areas.

Explain to each manager the "new agenda." Expenses that are not necessary cannot be tolerated. The company must remain strong and competitive. Assure the staff that no one will be punished for past excesses, but that each department will be, without question, responsible for and accountable for their own expenses.

Request from the accounting department a list of all the expenses of the company for the past three months divided by department or by function. Review this list with each manager in a meeting which includes other managers. Ask the responsible managers for their input on how they plan to reduce costs in their area without curtailing production or efficiency.

Don't over-manage the meeting. Give your managers free rein to suggest even the most ludicrous ideas and then discuss the ideas as a group. You may discover that your own lieutenants can solve in hours problems that you have wrestled with for months.

Assure the managers that the exercise is not intended as a punishment for past sins (of management or the employees) or as a witch hunt for any one employee. The objective is to teach responsibility and accountability for costs at all levels of the company. If the exercise is performed with the proper attitude you should gain a valuable insight into the areas where the company can reduce expenses.

Making Auditing the Responsibility of Each Manager

Request that each manager carry the lessons learned back to the employees who report to them. The message is that the company must have responsibility for and **accountability** for costs at all levels.

The manager should explain to each employee:

Overhead has grown to include costs and expenses that are not necessary for the operation of the company. The "new agenda" is to identify these areas and reduce the excess and the waste. The results will help the company to remain competitive and to overcome its current difficulties.

We must all work together as a team and examine all of the costs and expenses of our department and consider the ways in which these can be reduced.

The managers should arrange to meet with their employees at least once a week for the first month. Employees should be assured that there is no intent to punish anyone for past excesses or other sins.

Managers must be frequently reminded that the objective of the exercise is to teach responsibility and **accountability** for costs at all levels of the company.

STEPS TO REDUCE EXPENSES

1. Meet with your managers and review, as a group, the current list of expenses for each department that are treated as overhead, and obtain their input on what expenses can be eliminated or curtailed.

2. Inform each manager that they are **responsible** and **accountable** for the expenses of their area.
3. Let each manager know that they must carry the message back to their employees and work their department as a team to carry out the mission.
4. Meet once each week with the group of managers to review the costs savings. Each time an expense is identified that can be eliminated or curtailed, a schedule should be agreed to for realizing the costs savings.

THE PROBLEM OF CHARGEBACKS

When the cash flow of a company is limited, the imbedded costs of doing business can strangle a troubled company.

For a service firm, these costs can include shipping, messengers, taxi services, and long-distance telephone charges. For a distribution or manufacturing firm, these costs can include freight, packaging, trucking, and insurance.

It is standard practice to incur these charges and then invoice the customer for the costs of the services. These costs are called "expenses," "handling," "shipping charges," "rebills," or "chargebacks." Some companies add a fixed percentage of profit or overhead to the cost before invoicing the customer. The advantage of accepting responsibility for the direct costs of these services and then invoicing the customer is the "profit" gained by inflating the additional overhead charged.

Service firms are perpetually concerned with overhead that is not attributable to a particular client, and those firms that are not concerned with these types of costs should be.

Not uncommon is the case of the office manager trying to play the detective, totalling the Federal Express bills and discovering that thousands of dollars a year of overnight packages were being sent by the firm without the costs being rebilled to the proper customer.

Product-based firms are not exempt from these types of problems. Annual freight bills for tens or hundreds of thousands of dollars that are not rebilled to the customer can significantly decrease a company's profits.

The problems with chargebacks are primarily that (1) they have a bad habit of growing more rapidly than the underlying revenue, and (2) those that are not, or cannot be, "rebilled" to customers become "overhead" to your company.

Specifically, chargebacks are problems for a troubled company because:

- The company is responsible for the charges;
- They increase your accounts payable;
- The tracking and rebilling of chargebacks are a bookkeeping nightmare and require extensive manual paperwork;
- The rebilling becomes part of your company's accounts receivable and is subject to the same delays in being paid that your invoices normally receive; and
- If your customers are experiencing financial troubles, you may be incurring a receivable of questionable value.

The Solution to Chargebacks

The easy solution to most of the problems attributable to chargebacks is to not have the costs billed to your firm.

Why use your company's credit when you can grow your business on your customer's good credit? Using your customer's direct-billing accounts reduces your accounts receivable and your accounts payable attributable to chargebacks and does not drain your company's cash flow.

Direct billing also eliminates a significant portion of the bookkeeping chore of tracking and rebilling expenses attributable to each client and usually reduces client inquiries about the service costs associated with chargebacks.

The more economically distressed your customer, the more important it is to use their charge accounts where possible and not your company's credit.

A Service-Based Example

At a consulting firm, which was experiencing a cash flow shortage, chargebacks accounted for four days a month of the bookkeeper's time and could represent as much as 25% of the firm's accounts receivable.

The firm was being confronted with payables that were overdue and chargebacks that had not been invoiced to clients. Compounding the problem, its overnight courier accounts and its travel agency were both calling daily regarding overdue payments. The firm was more than three months behind in allocating and rebilling chargebacks and yet the providers wanted to be paid or they would terminate service.

The problem was solved when, after consultation with their major clients, the firm began using the client's courier accounts (Federal Express, UPS, DHL, etc.) when sending overnight packages. It began using the prepaid airline tickets and hotel arrangements provided by the client's travel agency. It even started using the client's charge cards when making long distance telephone calls on their behalf.

Although the solution did not entirely eliminate chargebacks, it resulted in a reduction of at least two-thirds of the value of outstanding chargeback invoices and more than half of the volume.

The solution was a win-win-win for the troubled company, their customers, and their vendors. The customers were pleased because they knew exactly what they were paying for; the troubled company was able to continue providing services without the threat of interrupting service for want of an airplane ticket or messenger; and the vendors were pleased because they were being paid.

A Product-Based Example

A manufacturer had fallen behind in paying its freight carriers. The carriers refused to pick up shipments until past accounts were settled. The company had orders ready to ship, but no way to deliver them to the customer.

After being honest with one customer, the manufacturer found a solution. After hearing the firm's tale of woe, the customer told the firm to use its account with the same carrier. The manufacturer quickly discovered that many customers were willing to let it use their shippers and pay directly for any costs incurred.

The solution was a win-win for both the manufacturer and its customers.

> To reemphasize, the easiest method of solving most of the problems attributable to chargebacks is to not have the costs billed to your firm.

CHAPTER 4

CUTTING COSTS

REDUCING TRAVEL AND ENTERTAINMENT EXPENSES

Travel and entertainment (T&E) are expense categories into which many unrelated expenses are often allocated. It is also surprising how few companies spot-check or audit the expense reports submitted by their employees. Unaudited T&E offers a great opportunity for abuse and overspending and its reengineering can account for up to 20% of cash savings.

Auditing expense reports does not assume that you have dishonest employees, but the results will help in identifying potential abusers and highlighting those who are careless with paperwork. The audit may reveal areas where costs can be reduced and will have the effect of keeping most employees honest.

What to Look For When Auditing Expense Vouchers

Cases of the abuse of travel and entertainment expense are many. I will relate a few stories that illustrate the different types of problems to be aware of.

The sales manager who claimed the strand of freshwater pearls purchased with his corporate American Express card were a gift to a valued customer in Taiwan. An audit two years later revealed that the pearls were not purchased until a week after the manager departed Taiwan (not to mention the fact that bringing pearls to the Orient is like taking coals to Newcastle).

A recent series of cases involved Members of Parliament during the Mulroney government. More than 17 Members of Parliament billed the government for numerous personal and family expenses. The Speaker's Office initiated an inquiry into some of the expenses and, in many instances, the Member of Parliament was required to repay Parliament. In several cases, criminal charges were filed.

Upon winding up Parliament after the election of 1994, the Speaker's Office found that departing Members who had lost their seats made off with everything from fax machines to couches.

Kenneth Solomon, once a contender for CEO of the now-defunct U.S. accounting firm of Laventhol & Horvath, admitted in 1993 that he had defrauded his partners on at least 154 occasions between 1982 and 1990 by submitting false expense reports.[1]

The lessons to be learned from these stories are that even the most blatant and obvious abuse can go undetected if the company fails to perform regular spot-checks and periodic audits of T&E expenses.

Cash Advances

Then there was the vice president of sales who travelled frequently to foreign countries. He requested and was given cash advances of $500 to $2,000 per trip for expenses. Upon his return, he submitted expense reports requesting reimbursement for business expenses charged to his personal credit cards without including a credit for the cash advances he had received.

Two years later, when the vice president was questioned, he told the auditor he hadn't spent the cash advances so he had saved them for future trips. A full audit revealed $4,500 of cash advances not accounted for.

This type of problem can occur in companies which customarily give employees cash advances for travel, but don't check expense reports to see if the advance was properly accounted for.

Most firms would be well advised to reevaluate their policies for cash advances, but for the troubled firm this applies ten-fold. There are very few circumstances where cash advances should be given to employees. If your company does give an employee a cash advance, then at least audit the expense report.

Most employees who travel have personal charge cards and can easily use their personal cards for travel expenses. The company can reimburse them upon their return to the office and their submission of an expense report. This way the employee will usually have the reimbursement weeks before their personal credit card bill is due.

Nothing is more effective than a codified travel policy with fixed guidelines as to permissible costs and expenses. Fixed rates for reimbursement for meals, prearranged hotel room agreements with major chains, and corporate rates with car rental agencies will bring costs under control and reduce the chances for abuse.

> ### Is This Trip Necessary?
> It is important to insure that every trip has a purpose and a result. No trips should be permitted unless the purpose is part of the company's current strategic objectives.

Airline Tickets

Airline tickets can be easily reused, exchanged, or converted to cash. When business trips are cancelled or itineraries change, make certain that the unused airline tickets and travel vouchers are returned to the company.

Consider implementing a company policy where unused tickets not returned to the accounting department within ten days are charged to the employee.

Another problem is that employees can interfere with your company's attempts to get the lowest ticket prices. Employees will often insist on flying a particular airline to earn "frequent flyer" mileage. Do not permit this practice. Inform your travel agency that all employees must travel on the airline offering the lowest fare.

Taxicabs and Limousines

Taxicabs and limousines in many Canadian cities produce either a printout receipt with the date and cost of the trip with GST or the driver provides a handwritten receipt to the passenger. The expense reimbursement receipts are then stapled to the expense reports.

Audits and verification of these receipts in various companies have produced receipts filled in by employees for higher amounts for standard trips, and submissions for logs when employees were either on vacation or absent.

The employees may or may not have been dishonest, but the companies found substantial errors and overcharges. These are usually missed by traditional audit procedures that consist of simply adding up the total claims.

Corporate Charge Cards

A distribution firm issued corporate credit cards to each officer of the company. The bills for the credit cards were addressed to the attention of each card holder. The officers reviewed the monthly bill and submitted it to the accounting department to be paid directly.

An audit of the bills for a senior vice president included a purchase of $20 of gasoline for his company car — a legitimate expense. A careful examination of the statement revealed three additional purchases of gasoline on December 27 from the same gasoline station. When questioned, the officer said that he had "mistakenly" used the wrong credit card when purchasing gasoline for his children's cars who were visiting for the holidays.

Simply verifying the license plate number on the charge slips would have revealed that the company had been unknowingly paying to refuel the officer's three family cars for several years.

Travel Agencies

We have found travel agencies to be the most notorious for sending incorrect invoices. The agencies' computer systems often generated charges for tickets that were reserved, but not confirmed, and did not properly reflect credits for tickets or vouchers that were returned.

At one travel agency, airline reservations were "mistaken" for confirmed ticket purchases so frequently that we contacted the owner. Her investigation revealed that the airlines rewarded the agency's employees with bonuses paid on the first of every month based on the aggregate ticket sales for the prior month. The owner noticed that some of her employees issued tickets during the last week of the month (based on reservations by clients) and then issued credits for those reservations that were not confirmed the following week — after they had been paid their bonuses!

Like many business owners, because of a failure to audit, she was not aware of the business practices of her own employees.

Automobile Reimbursement Expenses

It is a worthwhile exercise to examine the travel expense vouchers submitted by employees and spot-check mileage and toll charges. Depending on your type of business and the frequency and type of travel required, it may be cost effective to replace reimbursements for time and mileage with a fixed monthly car allowance.

How to Detect Fraud and Abuse

The lessons to be learned from the previous stories are that a failure to spot-check and audit expense reports is far more expensive than you would expect. The cause of excess expenses is not always the fraud and abuse that we described in the examples, but you won't know how much your company can save until you look further.

There is no substitute for frequent random spot-checks on all invoices and regularly scheduled audits. The audits will pay for themselves either by the problems they reveal or by the effect that the practice of auditing has upon those you employ and those you do business with.

Don't implement procedures to punish your employees for past abuses, but do install the controls and checks necessary to reduce unnecessary expenses.

REDUCING EMPLOYEE TRANSPORTATION COSTS

Employee transportation can be a significant cost for many firms. More than one firm that we have examined has found they can reduce their transportation costs without impacting performance in the least.

Reimbursing Employees for Use of Personal Vehicles

Sometimes reimbursing employees for the use of their personal automobile for company business may have the unwanted result of increasing the amount of travel. This is because a fee based on Revenue Canada's allowance of 21¢ to 31¢ per kilometre is usually more than the "out-of-pocket cost of operating the vehicle."

Although the fee is called a "reimbursement," in some cases it should be called a "subsidy." Reimbursement at the "official" rate may have the unwanted side effect of creating an incentive for use of personal vehicles and cause the employee to overlook lower-cost alternatives.

An employee at a distribution company, when promoted from the warehouse to a desk job, accepted the new position without the usual zeal of a man receiving a promotion. I met with him to discover the cause of his hesitation and found he was pleased with the new job but was disappointed to learn that he would not be required to make a weekly trip to a supplier. The trip was about two hundred kilometres and for three years he had been reimbursed by the company $50 for each weekly trip.

A few months later, at the local pub, the employee was asked why he was so upset about not being able to drive to the supplier. He said that his car was a gas miser and only used $10 of fuel for the weekly trip. The extra $160 a month he received was used for the monthly loan payment on the car.

Since his replacement in the warehouse didn't own a car, the company reverted to using United Parcel Service (UPS) for the pickup. The weekly cost to the company was reduced to $14, including insurance. The savings benefit to the company was four additional hours of employee productivity and $26 per week of expenses. Afterwards, no one at the company could say why they hadn't been using UPS for the past few years.

> ### What about Company Vehicles?
> Many company vehicles are actually luxuries, being employee benefits, and are not necessary for the business. A troubled business must eliminate all vehicles not essential for the business. If the vehicle is owned by the company, then sell it.

Selling Company-Owned Vehicles

Since at some future date the company may be audited regarding its disposal of company assets, it is recommended to take the vehicle to a local dealer and ask the dealer for a written estimate of the value of the vehicle. Alternatively, purchase a copy of the *Red Book* or *Blue Book* available at most major bookstores in their automotive section, or through your lending institution.

This is the guide used by most car dealers and sales personnel and is a reliable source for court purposes.

For liquidation purposes, the safest bet is to sell a car for at least its wholesale value. This is considered a more realistic test of value and not an unfair disposal. Going through the process of selling vehicles via a newspaper ad can be long and arduous. Accept only money orders or bank drafts.

In many jurisdictions, you will be obligated to certify the road worthiness of the vehicle and file a report as to the value of the transaction so that the provincial government can collect appropriate sales taxes when the purchaser registers the car.

A wholesale sale with a dealer, especially if several cars are involved, is faster and easier.

Several times we have observed employees purchasing cars from the company with an arrangement for payments to be made over time through payroll deduction. The problem with this seemingly harmless scenario occurs when the employee later leaves the employ of the company, or is laid off. The employee may make countless promises to send weekly cheques for the car payments, but if they have moved away they may never be heard from again.

Even with a title to the car, the company's legal recourse may not be worth the cost of recovery. Without the title, the company will have no hope of recovery.

The troubled company cannot finance automobile purchases and there are many institutions that are already in this business. However, if the company is compelled to agree to payments over time, act like a bank and **do not transfer title for the vehicle to the employee until 100% of the payments have been made.**

Selling or Exchanging Leased Vehicles

If the vehicle is leased, discuss terminating the lease with the leasing company or perhaps trading the car in for a less expensive vehicle. Although the cancellation payments on many leases make breaking the lease prohibitive, the dealer may take a Mercedes 300 in trade for two new leases on Chevrolets and will smooth over any rough edges with the leasing company. The company may discover that prepaying several months of lease payments, to terminate a lease, can be less expensive than continuing for the term. See the section on *Leasing* in Chapter 5 for additional help in this area.

Lease costs are only one part of the total costs of operating the vehicle. In considering the cost savings of early lease terminations, don't forget to include the costs of operating a vehicle: insurance, fuel, maintenance, and repairs. Particularly in luxury cars, these costs may be significant.

Reducing Wear on Company Vehicles

Another method for reducing costs is to require that employees leave company vehicles at the office on evenings and weekends unless required for work. Wear and tear, mileage, and maintenance can be reduced, and your automobile insurance carrier may reduce your premiums as a result.

Reducing Vehicle Insurance Costs

Insurance for company-owned vehicles can be very expensive. These policies should be reviewed at least annually to determine if costs can be reduced. Don't underinsure, but do examine your policy costs and coverage closely.

1. Eliminate coverage for rented automobiles where the company credit card (American Express, etc.) provides coverage at no additional cost.
2. Reduce maximum limit of coverage where company has a general umbrella policy for catastrophic liability.
3. Increase the deductible for collisions or eliminate the coverage.
4. Review the list of employees insured and authorized to drive company vehicles. reduce the list to include only those with good driving records who need to use the vehicles for business.

REDUCING GENERAL INSURANCE COSTS

A company should examine all of its insurance coverage (property and casualty, liability, workers' compensation, business interruption, travel, etc.) and costs at least every two years. Look closely at the business, at the insurance the company needs, and at the coverage the company can realistically afford.

Ask your insurance broker how the company can reduce costs, and request competitive bids from other agents. Insurance agents collect a commission for each dollar of premium paid; therefore, there is an economic disincentive to recommend a lower-cost policy when the customer appears satisfied.

Your broker's apparent complacency doesn't mean he needs to be replaced, but always remember — let the buyer beware. Shop around and make certain that the company has the proper insurance coverage and is getting the best coverage for its premium dollars.

Obtaining Copies of All Insurance Policies

Be certain the company has copies of every insurance policy for which premiums are being paid. Insurance agents are not always as diligent as they should be in sending updated or revised policies, and even when they do, these rarely used documents can easily become mislaid.

Include in the list of policies any insurance coverage the company has by virtue of its membership in a trade or industry association or corporate credit card program (American Express, VISA, Mastercard). Don't forget to include shipping insurance (Federal Express, United Parcel Service, etc.). Automobile clubs (CAA, provincial motor league) traditionally have included coverage for their members for vehicle breakdowns, towing, bail bonds, trip interruption, etc.

Maintenance Contracts and Warranties

Maintenance contracts are similar to insurance policies; some have provisions for the loss replacement of equipment that are triggered under specific conditions. Equipment that is usually covered by maintenance contracts includes computers, forklifts, telephone systems, facsimile machines, cellular telephones, pagers, copiers, postage machines, HVAC systems, burglar alarms and security systems, televisions, VCRs, machine tools, etc.

Included with most new equipment and some used equipment are manufacturer's or dealer warranties that may include de facto insurance coverage for repairs, premature breakdown, or fatigue. These types of "insurance" policies may also have been included with a roof repair or replacement, aluminum siding replacement, insect or pest extermination, landscaping, driveway paving, painting, carpet installation, insulation, basement waterproofing, or fence installation.

REDUCING TELECOMMUNICATIONS COSTS

Most firms do not regularly audit their telephone bills. Audits can be useful by revealing problems in employees' usage of the telephones, frauds committed by non-employees using the telephone lines (toll fraud), and areas where costs can be contained or reduced.

Although it can be a mammoth task to audit the bills, even for a small company, there are easy ways to achieve the desired results. The following methodology obtains results similar to those of a detailed audit without the need to hire extra staff for the accounting department.

Each Manager Has a Responsibility

Make auditing the responsibility of each manager. Request that managers explain to each of their employees the high cost of the personal use of business telephones and that no one will be punished, but the practice must stop. Explain that each department will be expected to review their monthly telecommunications bills and highlight any personal usage. Tell them the company expects payment from any employee who has more than $5 of personal calls in a month. The best way is to schedule a meeting in two weeks' time where the managers are to appear with the marked invoices.

Although the collection of monies owed may not be completely successful, don't be too concerned. The exercise is not intended as a punishment for past sins or as a witch hunt for any one employee. The objective of the exercise is to instill responsibility and **accountability** for telephone costs at all levels of the company. If the exercise is performed with the proper attitude, it will reduce the company's future telephone bills.

Tell managers the company is also concerned about the excessive use of directory assistance, which at 30¢ to 75¢ per call, can result in unnecessary charges of several dollars per employee, per month. Where significant use of directory assistance is found, call the telephone company and ask that they deliver a few telephone directories. At the next staff meeting give them to the manager whose employees regularly abuse the directory assistance service. The results will be very effective.

The following month, perform the same exercise. After three months, the telephone bills will have decreased an average of 25%

and the monthly responsibility can be assigned to the accounting department.

The same techniques detailed above are very effective in controlling and reducing the costs of cellular telephones and company telephone charge cards.

FOUR EASY STEPS TO REDUCE TELEPHONE COSTS

1. Inform employees the company will be auditing telephone bills.
2. Request that managers audit their departmental telephone bills.
3. Review the results of the audits at a monthly meeting.
4. Repeat steps 1, 2, and 3 once a month for three months.

Company Telephone Charge Cards

Audit and control of telephone charge cards is very poor for many firms. How many telephone charge cards have been issued in your company? Does the company have a complete list of the names of all card holders and corresponding account numbers?

In several firms we found telephone charge cards were issued and **renewed** for former employees who had not worked for the firm for over a year. Try recovering damages from an employee who used the card to charge $500 to $1,000 of personal telephone calls and now lives in another province.

Don't perform a witch hunt. Usually no one person is to blame for the past sins of management. Your objective is to reduce future costs and to instill responsibility and **accountability** for containing and reducing costs at each level of the company.

Obtain a list of all present and former employees who were issued telephone charge cards. Verify this list with the telephone service providers. Request that charge privileges be immediately terminated for anyone who is no longer an employee. Investigate any usage by former employees and try to carry out basic collection methods.

Another strategy is to inform employees that **all** telephone charge cards will be terminated at the end of the month and new cards will be issued. Request (in writing) all telephone service providers terminate all current charge cards. Issue new cards and have them distributed by the personnel department, along with a written statement of the policy for using the card. These terms should include a user's agreement: not to use the card for personal calls, to reimburse the company for any personal calls, and not to use the account after the termination of their employment with the company. Each employee should sign their acceptance of the terms and conditions before being given the card.

Cellular Telephones

Unless forced at gunpoint, never ever let anyone convince you to provide cellular telephones except to employees who **absolutely and positively** require them for business.

Suggest that employees purchase the telephones (even offer to share the cost of the unit) and agree to reimburse the employee for the monthly activation charge and for any calls made on company business. Cellular telephones can rapidly cost a company hundreds and even thousands of dollars per telephone, per month.

We know of a Toronto-based computer sales company which installed car phones for all sales and field personnel. Eight months later when individual bills were averaging $1,500 per month, the company reduced costs by replacing the cellular telephones with beepers.[2]

Request that the cellular service provide a detailed summary of the monthly bill and use the same technique as detailed in the prior section; ask employees to audit their own bills with copies reviewed by their managers.

Facsimile Machines

The invoices for the telephone lines used for facsimile machines are rarely audited. Don't depend on the audit trail of the fax machine as these can easily be erased and bypassed. One month, audit the telephone bills for the fax machines and observe any irregularities. It may be harder to find abuses with fax machines, but at least if the employees know that the company is looking at the bills then the fear of detection may serve as a deterrent.

We know of one firm where an employee regularly faxed the editorial cartoon from *The Globe and Mail* to her father in Europe. When asked if it wasn't expensive, she said, "Probably only $5 per call, but no one looks at the bill anyway."

Computer and Data Lines

Computer rooms and data communications lines can escape the watchful eye of even the best of auditors. More than once we have found active telephone lines installed for data communications applications being used for personal calls by otherwise honest and hard-working data processing employees. In two cases, the telephone lines had remained active and were used by employees for personal calls for years after the company's requirement for these lines no longer existed.

During the audit of the telecommunications costs, trace all voice, data, and leased lines ("circuits") that the company pays for. Verify all points of origin and destinations for the lines, and confirm that circuits are being used for their intended purpose.

Using Your Vendors' 800 Lines to Reduce Costs

One easy technique for reducing telecommunications costs is to make use of the toll-free lines provided by vendors. These numbers usually have 800 area codes or they are leased "tie lines" (also called "enterprise lines"), which provide a long-distance connection for the price of a local call.

Ask the manager of each department to list the names of the firms commonly telephoned by their subordinates and to research if any of the firms provides toll-free numbers. You will be surprised how many numbers your staff regularly call that have toll-free numbers. Call Bell or Unitel and ask for a copy of the 800 Directory that lists all toll-free service numbers sold by them.

Included in the list of firms with toll-free or local numbers are banks, insurance companies, airlines, hotels, car rental agencies, shipping companies, and many customer service lines. Why should the company pay for message units to wait twenty minutes on the line for an airline reservation, when using the airline's toll-free number costs the caller nothing?

If the company uses fax or modem data access to its vendors, don't forget that some vendors provide toll-free fax and modem numbers.

Compile a company-wide list of all commonly called contacts and their toll-free numbers. Distribute this list to all employees with a note encouraging them to use the toll-free numbers to reduce the company's telecommunications costs.

Using Fax Machines to Reduce Costs

Facsimile communication is a tool that can be used to communicate effectively and expeditiously with less ambiguity and at a lower cost than a voice telephone call. The average one-page letter sent by fax will take less than one minute to transmit.

Installing Your Own 800 Line to Reduce Costs

An Ontario domestic manufacturer had several hundred salespersons operating all over Canada, the United States, the Caribbean, and Europe. All of the salespersons telephoned the office several times each week and faxed sales orders. In analyzing telecommunications costs, the firm discovered it was paying for the salespersons' calls in one of three ways: reimbursing the salesperson for out-of-pocket costs, paying for the charges on the company-provided telephone charge card, or paying for collect calls to the office.

At the recommendation of its long-distance provider, the company installed a group of incoming 800 circuits that were toll free to the caller and would be billed directly at a bulk rate to the company. The salespersons were issued a list of toll-free numbers. Expenses could now be directly controlled from the home office and the cost of the average telephone call was reduced by 50%.

The implementation of its own 800 number program reduced costs and was so successful that within a few months the company installed a toll-free circuit for inbound facsimile communications to receive sales orders from the field.

Eliminating Answering Services

Many companies use answering services to receive calls when the receptionist is away from the telephone or the office is closed. For some firms the service is a question of image, for others, a necessity to allow emergency callers to reach them. These services can be eliminated by installing answering machines, with resulting savings of $50 to $100 per month.

Businesses that require emergency callers to reach them can include in the outgoing message a pager number for customers to call in case of an emergency.

Using Pagers

Pagers have become the most inexpensive and reliable method of maintaining contact while out of the office. These devices are significantly less expensive to use than cellular telephones and more reliable. With acquisition costs of $75 to $300 and monthly service fees of $5 to $50, pagers are an inexpensive method for replacing answering services and cellular telephones.

NOTES

[1]*The New York Times*, March 2, 1993, p.D-1, "Guilty of fraud? Try using too-frequent defense," Alison Leigh Cowan.

[2]A survey commissioned by *Inc.* on cellular telephone usage in 275 small to mid-size companies that issued car phones to their employees concluded that almost one-fourth of the companies felt that the company-provided telephones encouraged abuse, and many companies reported problems until controls such as expense ceilings were implemented. (*Inc.*, June, 1993, p.49, "Car Phone Pros and Cons.")

CHAPTER 5

MANAGING
PAYABLES

TAMING YOUR CREDITORS

Getting a handle on accounts payable problems can be difficult when the company is past due with most of its vendors and being harassed by telephone callers asking for payment. The daily calls can interfere with your business and have a demoralizing effect upon the employees who receive them.

The solution is to designate one or two persons in your company to receive all telephone calls from creditors. This simple approach will limit the interference and impact on morale.

One troubled company was significantly behind in paying its vendors. The accounting department and the receptionist were being bombarded by daily telephone calls from angry vendors. The vendors left lengthy messages detailing the invoice numbers, dates of purchases, the amounts past due, and threatened legal action or even worse!

For the receptionist the calls were time-consuming and interfered with her ability to answer other calls properly. And, knowing that no funds were available to pay vendors, all the accounting department could do was record the details of the call and verify the dates and amounts of past-due invoices.

We recommended the following approach to handle the irate vendors. The assistant controller was designated the contact person for all overdue accounts payable. A new telephone line

61

with direct (bypassing the switchboard) incoming access from the outside was installed in her office. The telephone had an answering machine attached which gave a pleasant greeting, inviting callers to leave a brief message, and advising them that the assistant controller would be in the office on Monday, Wednesday, and Friday afternoons and would respond to **all** messages received only on those days.

It required approximately two weeks to tame the angry vendors. Initially, vendors still attempted to reach the switchboard or the accounting department, but the receptionist always transferred the calls to the new accounts payable extension, where the caller heard the recording from the assistant controller's new answering machine.

On the designated afternoons, the assistant controller dutifully returned all telephone calls received. Although there was usually no substantive news to report to the vendor, they appreciated having their calls returned. The remainder of the company was now free to perform their jobs unimpaired.

Once you have "tamed" the problem of vendor harassment, the next step is to verify and correctly value the current accounts.

Verifying Accounts Payable.

Listings of accounts payable (AP) are usually fraught with errors. Before you can begin to make choices as to whom to pay and how much to pay, you need to have an accurate listing.

Errors creep into the AP listing in a number of ways. Common causes of errors are as follows: paying the same invoice twice, payments made but not recorded by the vendor, payments made but not recorded by your company, partial shipments being paid in full, returns to vendors not being recorded as credits, and errors in invoices received from vendors being left unchecked and entered into the AP system.

The company should never pay for products or services that were delivered damaged, failed to perform, or were not usable. Many computerized AP systems do not include the provision for placing a "hold" on paying an invoice because of problems with the merchandise or services.

Discovering later that the company overpaid a vendor during a month they were unable to meet payroll is a painful lesson to learn. When managing a company with insufficient cash flow, verifying the accounts payable will insure that the company pays only those invoices they owe.

If the task of verifying each invoice is too tedious, then at the least try to verify all invoices that are greater than $100.

Steps to Verify Accounts Payable

1. Generate a **complete** list of the accounts payable.
   - This list is one of the required items when filing for bankruptcy, so keeping it accurate and current is useful contingency planning.
   - The list should include each vendor's contact name, telephone and fax numbers, details for each unpaid invoice, an aging for each unpaid invoice, and details on any returned products or requests for credit.
   - Ask managers if there were any problems with any of the invoices (i.e., faulty products, partial shipments, backordered parts, incomplete or less than satisfactory service, or products which lacked merchantability).
   - Spot check the invoices against the company's purchase orders, shipping records, and warehouse receipts.
   - Audit where problems are uncovered with the spot checks.
   - Request credit (in writing) from the vendor for any problems discovered and obtain verification of the credit memorandum (in writing) from the vendor.

2. Call each vendor.
   - Verify each and every invoice in the list of payables.
   - Ask the vendor to send copies of any missing invoices.
   - Verify each payment made by the company during the last six months.
   - If the investigation reveals any discrepancies, then request the vendor produce copies of each invoice (and proof of delivery, if required) for the past six months.
   - Make all requests of vendors in writing.

During the verification of the AP, be careful not to commit to a payment schedule with any vendors. Let them know, without question, that the purpose of the inquiry is to verify the outstanding invoices, not to make promises about the future disbursement of funds. Without being too specific, tell vendors that the company is restructuring its finances and should be contacting them within two weeks to discuss outstanding invoices.

With an accurate list of payables, you can make decisions on which vendors to schedule for payments and for how much.

Why You Can Negotiate with Vendors

When a company is having problems meeting payroll and paying its monthly rent, owing $350,000 to a vendor that is 60 to 90 days overdue may seem like an insurmountable problem. Don't worry — most vendors are reasonable businesspersons. Think about how much your company and the vendor have in common.

Vendors want to be paid at least something. They want to keep your company as a customer and you can use this to your advantage when negotiating. Show them respect and talk to them. Vendors do not want to litigate to collect debts because (1) they might not win in court, and (2) they would lose you as a customer, and (3) litigation is a very lengthy process. But neither do vendors want to forgive and forget the entire amount that the company owes them.

Your company would like to pay the vendor as little as possible and to make these payments over an extended period of time. Your company does not want to suffer the harassment of an angry creditor or lose a relationship with a vendor that has taken several years to build. The common ground that exists between your company and your vendors is a big advantage in negotiating.

EXHIBIT 5-1

POINTS TO REMEMBER WHEN NEGOTIATING WITH VENDORS	
WHAT VENDORS WANT	**WHAT VENDORS DON'T WANT**
• To be paid something • To be treated with respect • Payments = Respect • To avoid litigation • To keep you as a customer	• To write off 100% of the debt • To be ignored • To wait forever to be paid • To litigate • To lose a future customer
WHAT YOU WANT	**WHAT YOU DON'T WANT**
• To pay as little as possible • To make payments over an extended period • To maintain vendor relationships • To avoid litigation	• To pay 100% of the debt today • Harassment by angry creditors • Unrealistic payment schedules • To litigate

The company does not have the funds to pay all creditors on a current basis, so you will need to examine each creditor on an individual basis. Then choose a plan of action based on the creditors' positions and the company's present and future needs for them.

CATEGORIZING YOUR CREDITORS

Divide creditors into four categories. The first category ("vital"), the highest priority, is limited to payments required on a regularly scheduled basis for the business to continue. Extended payment terms can still be negotiated, but your flexibility is limited. Vital payments can include current payroll, insurance, utilities, taxes, professional fees, rents (sometimes), and lease payments (sometimes). The remaining three categories ("A", "B", and "C") are based on the company's present and future needs for each vendor's goods or services.

A vendor that provided asphalt for the driveway will be in a low category for receiving payments, for the company is unlikely to need additional asphalt in the next 12 months. The United Parcel Service and the telephone company are vendors which the company needs on a daily basis and for which there are no alternative suppliers. They would receive a high ranking in the priority of vendors to be paid.

However, care should be taken to avoid problems with vendors who are in a position to assert a mechanics or other form of "automatic" lien on the company's property for nonpayment of an invoice.

Rank all vendors based on the company's future need to continue doing business with them. The "A" list are high priority suppliers. These vendors provide products or services that the business depends on and typically they are the sole sources for these goods. For example, if the company is primarily a dealer of RCA televisions, this list includes RCA.

The "B" list includes suppliers that provide goods that the company requires for the business, but that can be purchased from other sources. For the example of the car dealership, this list would include tire manufacturers and petroleum product distributors, of which there are several alternative suppliers.

The "C" list are suppliers either not unique in their pricing or in the services they deliver, or are those the company will not be needing in the next year. Examples would be a janitorial service, an office supply dealer, or the roof repair service. All of these suppliers can be replaced by another vendor with similar pricing.

Vendors on the "A" list deserve the most attention. You need to concentrate your efforts on negotiating with these vendors a payment schedule that both the company and the vendor can live with.

Vendors on the "B" list include many that can be negotiated with. The company has leverage over "B" vendors because they will not require them in the future. If "B" vendors are willing to work with the company through the troubled times then they may receive some payments. "B" vendors that won't work with the company quickly become a member of the "C" list. Vendors on the "C" list are unlikely to receive any payment until the company has stabilized its financial condition.

VENDOR CATEGORIES

1. Vital Payments: Current payroll, insurance, utilities, professional fees, and some rents and lease payments
2. "A" List Vendors: Sole source suppliers
3. "B" List Vendors: Multiple source suppliers
4. "C" List Suppliers: No longer necessary

Analyzing Each Vendor's Negotiating Position

When analyzing each vendor and planning the approach to negotiate monies owed them, consider the following factors: their willingness to work with the company during this troubled period, their size and sophistication, the amount the company owes them, and indirectly, the priority (for receiving payment) they would receive in a bankruptcy filing or insolvency proceeding.

Vendor's Willingness to Work with You   Business is business, but a vendor's willingness to be understanding and flexible during a troubled period can be very valuable to the cash-starved company. A vendor, owed payment on long-overdue invoices, who agrees to continue to make small shipments of critical goods necessary to maintain your business, has shown a willingness to work with the company during a troubled period and may deserve some favouritism in being paid.

Size and Sophistication   A vendor with total accounts receivable of $200 million may be less concerned with the company's debt of $200,000 than a small local vendor to whom $900 is owed. This is particularly true if the vendor needs the $900 to pay their own rent.

By "concerned" we mean the vendor's patience before litigating, their willingness to forgive a portion of the debt, and their willingness to negotiate an extended payment schedule.

Large and sophisticated creditors are more willing to negotiate a reduction in the total amount owed. Despite their protests that they have "never done this before," they are usually very experienced at negotiating these types of "adjustments." They will know the pitfalls of litigation and although they will be the first to threaten, they will wait the longest before initiating legal action.

Smaller and unsophisticated creditors are less likely to negotiate and may argue that even a 10% reduction in the amount owed would be unfair to them and unacceptable.

Amount the Company Owes   Most small vendors will not begin to litigate for amounts less than $1,000, and most of the company's larger creditors will not litigate for amounts less than $10,000. But **beware:** there are exceptions to this rule.

Try to estimate the amount of leverage that the company has over the vendor. The maxim which was repeated frequently at the time of Donald Trump's troubles and again during the continuing saga of the Olympia & York bankruptcies was that if you owe the bank $1 million you have a big problem, but if you owe the bank $100 million, then the bank has a problem! I would add another level; if you owe the bank $10 million, then both of you have a problem.

During a difficult period for your industry, even a relatively small debt of $25,000 to $50,000 can be very significant to a vendor. The more significant the debt is to a vendor, the more leverage you should have in negotiating. The objective of negotiations is to achieve a reduction in the total amount owed and extended payment terms in exchange for a promise of regular payments.

The company may also have leverage with a vendor by its market position. Your company's strategic importance to the vendor translates to leverage when negotiating.

For example, if your company is a manufacturer's only distributor in Alberta, then you are of strategic importance to the manufacturer until they find a replacement. This value is your leverage when negotiating. It may be less expensive for the manufacturer to be flexible and to work with the company during the troubled period than to recruit and build a relationship with a new distributor.

Influence that the Vendor Has   A vendor whose president is also on the board of the bank that holds a loan you have defaulted on, or a vendor who is influential with other members of your industry, may warrant special treatment.

Priorities the Creditor Would Have in Bankruptcy   Although you may not be planning to file for bankruptcy in the near future, a troubled company should always be cognizant of a creditor's potential standing in a bankruptcy court. Is the creditor's claim secured or unsecured? Would they have a priority to receive payment under the Bankruptcy and Insolvency Act?

There are two reasons why it is important to know a creditors potential priority in bankruptcy: (1) if the situation worsens, they may try to force you into an involuntary bankruptcy, and (2) if you are ever in bankruptcy you want to know the effect of having paid them today.

Creditors who could force you into bankruptcy deserve special attention. You do not want to anger them and you may opt to withhold payment from others in favour of those who would receive a priority in bankruptcy.

HOW TO NEGOTIATE WITH VENDORS

The objective when negotiating with vendors is to gain and to retain as much flexibility as possible. Stay in telephone contact with your vendors and let them know who is managing the relationship. Don't let them be the leader. If they start calling every day, tell them clearly and firmly that you will speak to them every Thursday. Vendors are rarely incorrigible and are usually easy to train. Remember the example of the accounts payable manager who put a message on her answering machine that she would be in Disneyland for a week and received no complaints when she returned.

Before contacting each vendor, review your negotiating position. Write down those elements of the company's relationship with the vendor that give you additional leverage. Remember the commonality of interest that you share with the vendor. Use both the company's leverage and any common ground as tools for negotiating.

Don't reveal to the creditor your entire tool belt in the first telephone conversation. Generally, you would like to "stretch" the negotiating process out over several weeks. The more time that elapses while you are in the negotiation phase, the more time you or others in your company will have to effect a recovery of the business before having to pay any part of the debt.

Don't Worry about Litigation

The troubled company should avoid litigation where possible and always **appear** to be concerned about the threat of creditor lawsuits. However, never forget that the leverage in negotiating is *when the creditor stops talking and initiates litigation, they have lost.* Assuming that you have only flimsy defenses for nonpayment, the **absolute minimum** time required from the initiation of a suit to the creditor receiving a judgement, in most provinces, is from six to twelve months!

Don't forget, there is also a possibility that the creditor will get their day in court and lose their case or receive only a partial judgement.

During the time that a creditor's lawsuit is winding its way through the legal labyrinth, your company will be growing financially stronger, and the creditor will be spending money to prove their case while still waiting to be paid.

You don't need to educate the company's vendors in the pitfalls of litigation, but if they go over the edge, then try the following approach: tell the creditor their choice is unfortunate, the outcome in court is not a certain judgement, and that with some additional patience they might do better by standing with you during these troubled times. Ask the creditor to consider your offer and agree to telephone them in a week.

Most creditors will bluff several times before initiating litigation; its your job not to let them fall out of the ring. Always leave creditors room to return to the negotiating arena. You can play hardball later.

NEGOTIATING WITH DIFFERENT CATEGORIES OF VENDORS

Vital Payments

These are payments that absolutely and positively (with apologies to Federal Express) must be paid regularly, in full, for the company to remain in business. A few vendors categorized as vital can be convinced, from time to time, to accept payments under terms and conditions similar to those on the "A" list. However, unlike "A" vendors, the terms granted by vital vendors are usually a one time forbearance, for one week, or one month.

You have some flexibility with vital payments, but not much. You can usually negotiate the following types of arrangements: spreading (or financing) of annual insurance premiums into quarterly or monthly payments, spreading a monthly rental into weekly payments, or deferring payment of a large commission cheque into several partial payments.

"A" List Vendors

The objective in negotiating with vendors on the "A" list is to agree mutually to write off a portion of the debt in conjunction with an agreement to stay current with all new invoices and to make payments on the balance due over an extended period.

Paying $150,000 at one time may be too much, but negotiating to be forgiven for $70,000 of the debt and to pay the balance of $80,000 in ten monthly instalments may be manageable and acceptable. (Your leverage is that they want to be paid something.)

Use your leverage that they are willing to accept a reduction in the debt and have a vested interest in your remaining in business. Tell the vendor that as much as you would like to pay the entire debt, doing so would put you out of business, which wouldn't benefit either of your firms. Wouldn't a fresh start, where you would agree to remain current on all future invoices, benefit both of you (using common interests and the leverage that they want to keep you as a customer).

"B" List Vendors

Vendors on the "B"list are those that you can replace, though not necessarily without some external costs. If vendors show a willingness to work with your company during its troubled period and continue to do business with you, then they deserve your respect. Try to allocate some funds to make token payments to these vendors. Even nominal payments will be received favourably because they show your respect (remember: Payments = Respect) for the vendor.

When making payments to "B" vendors, always send them to the attention of a particular individual. The company may have a lock box or a P.O. box for accepting payments, but don't use it. Your purpose in making a payment is more to show your respect than to make a significant dent in the total debt owed to the vendor.

Another reason for sending payments to an individual's attention instead of to a lock box is the extra one to two days of "float" before the cheque is deposited in, and clears, the bank.

Make the payment a personal gesture between two businesspersons. Telephone the recipient and inform **them** you are sending a payment. It's a small payment, but you want **them** to know you are making a strong effort under difficult circumstances.

If the vendor cannot be persuaded to agree to terms acceptable to the company's current financial position and refuses to continue doing business with you, then relegate them to the "C" list. Continue negotiating with them, but pay them nothing!

EXHIBIT 5-2

PRIORITIZATION OF ACCOUNTS PAYABLE					
DESCRIPTION OF PAYMENT		PAYMENT PRIORITY			
		VITAL	A	B	C
Payroll and Commissions	**Current**	Yes			
	Past Due				✓
Pension Funding					✓
Vacation Pay					✓
Withholding Taxes		Yes			
Corporate Taxes	**Federal**	Negotiate	✓		
	Provincial	Negotiate	✓		
	Local	Negotiate	✓		
Secured Creditors					
Mortgages		Negotiate	✓	✓	
Loans		Negotiate	✓	✓	
Leasing Companies	**Vehicles**	Negotiate	✓	✓	
	Equipment	Negotiate	✓	✓	
Unsecured					
Rent		Negotiate	✓	✓	✓
Insurance		Negotiate	✓		
Utilities		Negotiate	✓		
Professional Fees		Negotiate	✓		
Travel & Entertainment			✓	✓	✓
Freight, Fedex, UPS, etc.		Negotiate	✓	✓	
Vendors					
"A" List Vendors			✓		
"B" List Vendors				✓	
"C" List Vendors					✓

"C" List Vendors

The only purpose in negotiating with vendors that you have relegated to this category (Arlo Guthrie's proverbial Group "W"
bench) is to avoid the nuisance and cost of your company defending multiple small law suits. The company may eventually
be in a position to pay some of these vendors, but not today and
not for the next few months.

"Nice Guys Finish Last"
Leo Durocher, Yankee Coach and Player (1906-91)

As much as you may be sympathetic to the plight of vendors
relegated to the "C" list, never forget that your company is
fighting to stay alive.

In the recovery mode you cannot afford to do any favours
(i.e., make any payments) to vendors unless you need the
vendor's cooperation to survive.

Any favours that you grant this month may come at the
expense of your own paycheque next month!

LEASES

Leases can be grouped into three basic categories based on the
type of asset being leased: vehicle, equipment, or real estate.
Also of importance is whether the lease is an obligation of the
corporation, or if an officer or employee cosigned (guaranteed
or accepted joint responsibility) for the obligation.

If an individual accepted **joint responsibility** for the lease,
then the lessor would have the right to recover from both the
company and the individual in the event of a default or for any
damages sustained by early termination of the lease.

If an individual **guaranteed** the lease, then the lessor could
recover damages from the individual **only** after the lessor had
failed in their attempts to collect from the company. Some leases
have provisions which bring the guarantee into force immediately upon a default of certain terms of the lease.

Ask the company's lawyer to review each of the leases and to
identify the responsible parties and the order and trigger conditions for each obligation. An analysis of obligations and guarantees relating to leases is also necessary in order to understand the
effects of a potential bankruptcy filing or insolvency proceeding.

Vehicle Leases

Why are lenders holding vehicle leases difficult to negotiate with and reluctant even to begin negotiations? The reasons for their position are simple: why should they negotiate? They have good security and usually have additional recourse against individuals in the company.

The security for the lease, the vehicle, has a ready market, therefore the lessor could take possession of the vehicle and either sell or lease it again. Any damage to the vehicle (their security) is covered by required insurance. Most vehicle leases for small and medium-sized businesses require that an officer cosign or guarantee the obligation. This means that if the company defaults on the lease, the lessor would have legal remedies against others.

Therefore, given the lessor has reliable security and more than one pocket to go after, these lenders are the least likely to negotiate better terms, but there are still ways to tame them.

Taming Vehicle Leases

1. If the vehicle has recurrent service problems, and the company leased it through a dealer, there may be recourse available under provincial or federal law to withhold lease payments until the vehicle is "satisfactorily" repaired.

2. Most dealers conduct their leasing under a separate company or sell the lease to a finance company within a few days or months. The dealer may tell you that their sale of the lease, to a finance company located 2,000 miles away, relieves them of any obligation. However, the contract under which they sold the lease to the finance company, or the laws in your province, may not support them. Ask legal counsel to review the terms of the company's leases for any options or recourse the company may have for vehicles that have not performed as promised.

3. Before negotiating with the lessor, decide what the company would like to do with the leased vehicle. The options are to return the vehicle to the lessor, transfer the obligation to another company, transfer the obligation to an individual, exchange the vehicle for alternate transportation, sell the vehicle, pay the lease cancellation fees, purchase the vehicle.

4. Don't be under the mistaken belief that because the lease terms say that the lease is not assumable and the

company is not free to sell the vehicle that your company is limited in its options. Just because it is written in a contract doesn't mean that a lender will not agree to these types of arrangements. When faced with the prospect of chasing the monthly payments and possibly repossessing the underlying security through the legal system, a lessor may be very willing to accept a new lessee or agree to the sale of the vehicle to a third party.

5. Prove to the lessor that it is to their advantage (this probably won't work). Be forceful, tell them the choice is to let the company "off the hook" and accept revenue today from a new source or learn to be very patient waiting for payments. Don't tell the lessor to begin collection procedures. They know their job and if they don't, it's not to the company's advantage to educate them. If you are reasonable, but firm, the lessor may exhibit some flexibility.

WARNING

If the lessor has agreed to alternate terms and conditions, always confirm the proposed understanding in writing, but never assume obligations without consulting legal counsel.

Be particularly careful when a lessor releases the company from an obligation. The release must also extend to any individuals or entities with joint responsibility for, or who acted as guarantors for, the company's performance under the lease.

Returning the Vehicle to the Lessor Try to reach a mutual agreement before returning a vehicle to the lessor. The company does not need to have agreed to all of the terms under which the vehicle is being returned, but the company's position in a legal proceeding may be more defensible if the lessor has agreed to take possession of the vehicle.

We have heard of situations where lessees have returned vehicles by driving the vehicle onto the front lawn of the lessor, locking the car, and leaving with the keys. You may have heard the news story about the man who left the vehicle in the lessor's lobby after crashing through a plate glass window! The lessor had refused to renegotiate the expiration date of the lease. Although these methods may give personal satisfaction, it is not a recommended approach.

W A R N I N G

Upon return of the vehicle, the lessor may "discover" damage, excessive wear and tear, or other problems. To protect the company, before returning the vehicle take complete and close-up colour photographs of the vehicle, both the inside and outside, and retain these along with a full copy of all service records.

Consider paying a dealer in the next town a nominal $25 to $100 fee to give a written appraisal of the value of the car, noting any damage or excessive wear. Keep this appraisal confidential and do not reveal its existence to the lessor.

Should the lessor seek a legal remedy to recover additional monetary damages for the poor condition of the vehicle, the company will have a strong defense with a written appraisal from an independent dealer and detailed colour photographs.

Transferring the Obligation to another Company   Can the company transfer the lease to another related or unrelated concern that can use the vehicle? To the parent company or another division? Do you know another company that needs and could use the vehicle? Even if the company is required to pay a few months of the lease payments to have another company assume the obligation, it may be worthwhile to reduce the liabilities of the company or to release the guarantors of future responsibilities.

Transferring the Obligation to an Individual   Perhaps the employee who drives the vehicle wants to assume the lease obligation or purchase the vehicle. People become overly attached to the vehicles they drive daily and you can use this emotional attachment to the company's advantage.

Exchanging the Vehicle for More Suitable Transportation   If the company leased the vehicle from a dealer, they may have additional options available. Dealers make money through leasing in two ways: first by the profit on selling the vehicle to the finance company, and second by receiving a commission on the lease (an additional 1% to 5% of the sale price!). **Use the dealer's profit incentives to your advantage.**

Example: a troubled company needs to replace its aging delivery van, but cannot afford the additional leasing costs. Last year the company leased a luxury Cadillac for the vice president of sales. The company should consider returning to the same dealer and offering to "trade in" the luxury car for new leases on a van and a Chevrolet. Although the terms of the lease may not allow a trade-in and the company may incur additional charges, the dealer may accept the offer.

The dealer has the incentives of profit on two new vehicle sales and the commission on two new leases to convince them that the trade is in their best interest. The dealer can use their influence to persuade the finance company to allow the "trade-in" and the troubled company will receive better value for its lease dollars.

Another value of downsizing from luxury to moderate automobiles is the benefit to the public image of the troubled company. A company executive driving a luxury car does not set the correct image. Consider the effect of a manager seen driving a luxury car has on the workforce that recently accepted salary and benefit reductions to help the company survive.

Selling the Vehicle   If the company has paid for more than half the term of the lease, it may be advantageous to find a buyer for the vehicle and approach the leasing company with the potential purchaser. Propose a "deal" to the lessor and demonstrate it is to their advantage to permit the sale. **Remember: always use your leverage.**

Paying the Lease Cancellation Fees   Cancellation fees are the contractual stipulated costs that the company would pay to return the vehicle and the keys to the lessor without any continuing obligation. These fees can vary greatly and can range from two months payments to the full value of the remainder of the lease. Don't be shy — explore the possibility and examine the lease or ask the company's legal counsel, or the leasing company, what "official" options (i.e., before negotiating) are available.

Purchasing the Remainder of the Lease   Leases often include a purchase option at expiration. Depending on the value of the vehicle and the terms of the lease, it may sometimes (though rarely) be advantageous to prepurchase the remainder of the lease to obtain title. The company would then have the option of selling the vehicle to recoup the cash value of the asset.

Equipment Leases

Leases are often a convenient method of financing the acquisition of equipment such as computers, photocopiers, mail room machinery, closed-circuit TV camera systems, security systems, telephone PBXs, generators and vending machines. One reason these types of equipment are leased is that the leasing is often provided by a financial subsidiary of the manufacturer. The leases are offered at preferential interest rates with little or no down payment.

The relationship between the manufacturer and the leasing company is leverage the company can use to its advantage in terminating or renegotiating the terms of equipment leases. The company may be able to sell the equipment back to the manufacturer, or use it as a trade-in for another piece of equipment.

Telephone the manufacturer, explain to them the situation and terminate the lease. Suggest to the manufacturer that they pick up the equipment or ship it back to them. Legally the leasing company probably has recourse to recover the remainder of the lease value or a cancellation fee, but manufacturers are typically more interested in recovering the equipment than chasing a troubled business for a few months of payments. Once they have the equipment, they can sell it to another customer.

S U G G E S T I O N

The close relationship that exists between leasing/selling/ receiving companies can significantly influence the approval terms on new leases. Many a troubled business, no longer able to borrow elsewhere, has found it surprisingly easy to lease a new photocopy machine with an annual service contract.

CONTRACTUAL LIABILITIES

Other contractual liabilities that need to be renegotiated when reducing or terminating an operation can include uniform delivery and laundry contracts, janitorial contracts, waste removal contracts, maintenance contracts, telephone answering services, security services, and blanket purchase orders. Although some of these businesses will initiate litigation to recover the damages incurred in early terminations of contracts, most will be reasonable and negotiate.

For some unknown reason, answering services and uniform delivery services are notorious for initiating litigation to collect paltry amounts for early terminations of contracts.

Janitorial and waste removal contracts can be difficult to terminate unless past-due invoices are paid. They will send "heavyweights" to a company to collect unpaid invoices and may not be willing to negotiate if the company waits until they are three months behind before terminating the agreement. Inform them early that the company is having "difficulties" before it becomes a problem. Sol Stein in *Bankruptcy* even says that from his research he was told that "Others will counsel in a whisper to let the garbage man double up on payments till he's caught up."[1]

NOTES

[1]*Bankruptcy: A Feast for Lawyers*. Sol Stein, M. Evans and Company, Inc., 1989/1992, p. 14.

CHAPTER 6

MANAGING RECEIVABLES

RECEIVABLES are those funds that would flow into the company's coffers were the business to continue normal operations (i.e., your cash flow). Receivables can include payments by customers (traditional accounts receivable), refunds from tax authorities, insurance settlements, credits and overcharges from vendors, rents, royalties, lease payments, and proceeds from sales of assets. Each receivable requires a different management and collection strategy. The first distinction is between receivables due from customers and other receivables.

RECEIVABLES FROM CUSTOMERS

Similar to the approach when taming the payables problem, a priority for a troubled business is to assemble an accurate list of all accounts receivable (AR).

When compiling this list, it is also prudent to assemble a dossier on each customer. There are two reasons for the dossiers: (1) the company may want to sell the customer list and having a complete dossier will make the sale easier, and (2) if the company decides to give problem receivables to a collection agency, the dossiers will increase the likelihood of a recovery.

Pay particular attention to accounts that might have been written off or been marked uncollectible during the past 12 months. Collusion between the company's employees and customers can result in mysterious changes to receivables. Receivables from customers that were written off may also prove collectible when turned over to a collection agency or a lawyer who specializes in collection.

An invoice representing goods or services that were delivered to the customer will often be marked uncollectible because there was a misunderstanding with the customer, and the salesperson responsible for the account did not want to interfere with a future business relationship. If the company is terminating the operation, they are unlikely to have a future business relationship with the customer and, with "no holds barred," a collection agency or lawyer may find the debt collectable in part, if not in whole.

The AR can easily contain errors, omissions, and inaccuracies. All invoices for the past twelve months should be compared to documents such as the purchase orders and shipping manifests to substantiate their accuracy. Cross-checking the accounts receivable with other documents may point to potential fraud, and unknown (or hidden) assets can be revealed.

A wholesale distributor terminating an export division discovered many pieces of equipment priced at $5,000 to $25,000 each with a total market value of almost $500,000 not fully accounted for. Each piece of equipment had been shipped to customers as "demonstration models" or "samples" over the past three years, without any receivable being generated. No obvious fraud was revealed, but after invoicing the customers for these "samples," the company received $140,000 of payments and the return of $190,000 of merchandise. This amounted to a recovery rate of approximately 66%! How much higher would the recovery rate have been if management had reviewed accounts receivable every six months?

Collecting Receivables from Customers

The approach that a company needs to take with respect to its receivables from customers depends on the path that it has chosen for that segment of the business. The plan has two components: the **strategy** and the **desired result**.

COLLECTIVE CUSTOMER RECEIVABLES		
SURVIVAL PLAN	STRATEGY	DESIRED RESULT
Increase	☎ **Negotiate**	✛ **Dovetail**
Reduce	☎ **Negotiate**	✈ **Accelerate**
Sell	✓ **Collect**	✂ **Discount**
Terminate	✓ **Collect**	✂ **Discount**

SURVIVAL PLANS

Increase Revenues

If the plan for the business is to concentrate upon and increase that portion of the operations to which the receivables relate, then use your current receivables as leverage to grow your business.

Inform your present customers of your plans and encourage them to include your group of products and services in their future purchases. Use your marketing skills!

Negotiate with the customer and **"dovetail"** any invoices due from the customer with new invoices for additional goods and services. Consider promotions such as offering customers special discounts for new orders when accompanied by prepayment.

Reduce Operations

When reducing or shrinking operations to reduce costs or increase profitability, there is a possibility that the result may alter and possibly damage existing relationships with customers and affect your future ability to collect on the receivables. This concern is genuine, when changing the nature of your business you should not expect that your customers will greet your changes with open arms.

Balance your schedule for reducing the business with your progress in negotiations with customers relating to current and past-due receivables. Your strategy should be to **negotiate** with the objective of **accelerating** the payments. The benefit is that if the customers react to the company's plans by withholding or delaying payments, the amount of receivables at risk will be reduced.

Sell the Company

The status of receivables (i.e., their value) when selling a business is a significant concern to both the buyer and the seller. If the buyer is concerned about the future ability to collect receivables, then they will discount their value. One possible reaction of the seller is to remove the receivables from the sale and to collect as much as possible prior to closing. If the buyer has confidence in the value of the receivables, they may demand that the entire list be included in the purchase. This can present a problem if a customer pays a receivable during the due diligence period (i.e., before closing).

No seller of a troubled business should ever give up cash in hand, and therein lies the dilemma. The only solution is to accept the fact that there will be minor adjustments to the purchase price of a business at closing.

Your mission in selling a troubled business is to maximize the cash you can legally take from the business prior to closing. Make every possible effort **to collect** outstanding receivables before the closing date.

Terminate All Operations

Terminating operations can be very hazardous to the health (collection) of your receivables. If you have made the decision to terminate a business, then move quickly to collect all of the accounts receivable, today. Do not delay and do not inform your customers of your decision to terminate until after your have collected the majority of your receivables.

Collect It Now!

When selling a business or terminating operations your strategy for collecting receivables is similar: collect them today. You may not have the ability to collect the monies in the future; therefore, even if collection today requires taking a substantial discount, it may be worth it. The following table summarizes the basic strategies for converting your receivables into cash in the bank.

HOW TO CONVERT RECEIVABLES INTO CASH

- Offer customers **discounts** of 20% for early payments.
- If a customer offers to mail you a cheque, suggest that you or someone else from the company will **personally** pick it up today (don't delay).

- For any receivables where a dispute exists with the customer, offer a compromise and split the difference.
- Don't be greedy, get the cash!

COLLECTING OTHER RECEIVABLES

Receivables can come from many sources other than your customers. Don't ignore all the other sources. Many a business has terminated operations only to discover six months or a year later that receivables existed of which they were not aware. **Examine all avenues for recovering monies due the company.**

Refunds and Credits

- Refunds from tax authorities such as GST
- Insurance settlements and overpayments
- Credits, overcharges, and reimbursements from vendors
- Co-op advertising and promotion credits
- Refunds for cancelled travel arrangements
- Royalties
- Rents and lease payments
- Reimbursements from employees
- Security deposits on utilities, real estate, equipment
- Deposits for mailing fees and postage meters
- Advance deposits for appearances in trade shows and conferences.

Refunds from Tax Authorities   Just because the company is behind on some tax obligations does not mean that all departments of the federal, provincial or municipal taxing authorities communicate with each other or are even aware of the delinquency. We have observed companies owing hundreds of thousands of dollars of past-due taxes requesting and receiving cheques from the government for tens of thousands of dollars of overpayments from prior periods. **If you don't discuss other taxes or periods, they may not even look for them.**

1. Make requests of taxing authorities in writing and keep them short and simple.
2. Do not mention any periods other than the period during which there was an overpayment or refund due.
3. Write a separate letter for each overpayment and request payment by cheque.

4. Do not allow past overpayments to be applied to future taxes.

Insurance Settlements and Overpayments   If the company is due any settlements for claims then negotiate and offer to take a small discount in exchange for a speedy disposition. If the company has made estimated insurance payments, but the business has decreased, request a refund.

Insurance overpayments are most common with unemployment and workmens' compensation insurance where the premium is based on a formula determined by the types of employees, their salaries and the total payroll. If the company reduced its personnel roster or salaries during the past two years, an updated census of your personnel should have been submitted to the insurance carrier. If the census has not been done, then do it today and include the effective date of each and every employment termination or salary reduction.

Request in writing, separately from each insurer, a cheque for each overpayment. Do not permit the overpayment to be applied to a future or past-due premium. The company needs the cash today!

Credits and Reimbursements from Vendors   Did the company return inventory or product to a vendor but not receive proper credit? Did the company make a duplicate payment for an invoice or overpay for goods? Do not delay; ask for payment today. Fax the vendor a letter requesting a cheque. Don't accept a credit unless you absolutely must. Explain to the vendor that your accounting system "cannot handle" a credit and you must receive a cheque to keep your records straight.... Try saying it, you never know. If the vendor hasn't read this book, it just might work to get you the money.

Is the company entitled to reimbursements from vendors for performing warranty repairs, special services or promotions? Be certain all claim forms have been submitted and request an expedited cheque, today. Again, ask for a cheque, not a credit against payables. Tell the vendor that reimbursements and purchases are handled by separate departments and that the company needs to receive a cheque to offset the receivable. Try saying it — it just might work.

Co-op Advertising and Promotional Credits   "Co-op" advertising and promotional credits are "earned" when the company sells products of a firm with a formal cooperative or marketing promotions program. Typically these programs reimburse the company for advertising and marketing efforts equivalent to 2% or 3% of sales of the manufacturer's products.

If the company owes the manufacturer money, they may be required to offset the amount owed, by the value in the co-op account. More frequently, these programs are being administered by independent service bureaus who administer co-op programs for hundreds of manufacturers, and you can request a cheque from them without even mentioning any amounts past due the manufacturer. A troubled business may be unaware that it is sitting upon thousands or tens of thousands of dollars of co-op funds.

Refunds for Cancelled Travel Arrangements Particularly if the firm is scaling back or terminating operations, they may have cancelled travel plans for which they purchased airline tickets, prepaid hotel arrangements, or booked conventions. Don't delay — request a cheque for the cancellation and submit all airline tickets directly to the airlines for reimbursement.

If the company is not eligible to receive refunds, try to sell the travel arrangements to another company. If these travel arrangements are related to a trade show or conference, advertise the prepaid arrangements in trade publications and the company will probably find a buyer.

Royalties, Rents, and Lease Payments If the company receives royalty or license payments, consider offering a discount for accelerated payments. If the company is receiving monthly royalties, offer to accept a discount for the licensee paying the next year's license fees or royalties in advance. If the company receives payments based on production quantities or quantities sold, offer to grant the payee a discount on quantity by making advance payments on the next six or twelve months of forecasted payments.

Reimbursements from Employees Check with the company's bookkeeping or human resources department. If current employees owe the company money, immediately start collection procedures. Give the employees ten days to make arrangements for repayment or start deducting from their next paycheque.

If past employees owe the company money, make a strong effort to collect. If the amount is greater than $500, initiate legal action to recover the funds.

Deposits

Deposits on Utilities   Has the company terminated leases or vacated properties during the past three years? If so, did the company receive all of the security deposits due on utilities? **Request these deposits today.**

If the company has terminated telephone services or reduced the number of lines at a facility, they may have an excess amount on deposit as security for payment. Don't worry that the company owes money on other bills to the same utility. Utilities are like taxing authorities when it comes to refunds. Utilities can be litigating to collect monies on one account and issue a refund cheque on another account, even where both accounts have the same service name and address.

Deposits for Mailing Fees   If the company does frequent mass mailings, uses a business reply mail permit or a postage meter, they are required to deposit sufficient funds to cover several months of expected usage. The company won't receive refunds on these deposits unless you ask for them.

Several times we have been involved in the search for deposits at the post office with profitable results. Joan Cook, an insolvency case we worked on, who was once a leader in the mail-order business, filed for bankruptcy in early 1992. Several months later, the chief financial officer "remembered" about a $70,000 deposit with the post office, which was recovered for the benefit of creditors. Unfortunately, these funds should have been available to the company prior to terminating operations, not afterwards.

Advance Deposits for Trade Shows   The company may be entitled to refunds for advance deposits on trade shows and conferences. Or they may be able to sell the registration or display space to another company. Advertise the space in trade publications and you will probably find a buyer.

Other Deposits   Many other services require security deposits. Don't ignore these deposits. You won't see them if you don't request them. Include in this list: deposits on vending machines, LP gas containers, garbage and recycling dumpsters, pagers, and cellular telephones.

LOOK EVERYWHERE FOR ASSETS

Examine all possible avenues for recovering assets when terminating business operations.

With company-owned equipment (or other company assets) in the personal possession of employees, try to sell the assets to the employees at "fair market value." If the company requests the equipment but it is not returned, don't hesitate to hold back a payroll cheque due the employee until the property is returned. If the company is terminating an employee, they may not feel any obligation to return property. The employee may even feel a grudge against the company which, in their own mind, justifies the conversion of company property to their own.

We have observed cars, computers, fax machines, cellular telephones, pagers, VCRs, colour televisions, paper shredders, handtrucks, tools, software, books, and cameras disappear because of failure to ask for their return, or the failure to request the return at the proper time (i.e., before the last payroll or commission cheque is issued).

CHAPTER 7

TERMINATING AND REDUCING OPERATIONS

THE "IMAGE" PROBLEM

For most entrepreneurs it is easier to start a new business than to terminate or reduce existing operations. The reasons are purely machismo and ego. Those who view terminating operations as synonymous with defeat must remember that the primary objective in a rescue mission is to stabilize the company's financial position. It is usually neither profitable nor feasible for the company to maintain all of its current operations while recovering from its troubles.

An unprofitable real estate brokerage may not have enough business to support two office locations, but could be profitable when paying the overhead of one location. The closing of the second office is not a defeat. It is a prudent and necessary business decision. Once the decision has been made and the termination completed, the brokerage's deteriorating financial condition will be stabilized and the first objective of its recovery will have been achieved.

The Image of Success

When terminating or reducing operations, do not confuse the image of success with the need to return a company to financial health. If the company needs to sell the Mercedes or the airplane to pay the bills, don't hesitate. If the company needs to close its offices and move to less expensive space, do it today and start counting the money saved.

Many entrepreneurs get caught up in "looking successful" instead of managing a company through difficult times to remain profitable. Don't worry about how successful your neighbour or competitor is. Your neighbour may look successful, but don't be surprised if their "image of success" is a lifestyle beyond their means.[1]

> If the future of the company is important to you, then don't hesitate to do what is necessary to save it.

Saving a business may require reducing the company's operations and curtailing expenses or even selling part of the business, but if that is what it takes to succeed, then don't falter in your steps. Play to win!

Although bankruptcy no longer carries with it the nineteenth-century stigma of failure, it is a better image to be a moderately profitable entrepreneur then a formerly flamboyant and now bankrupt debtor.

A GUIDE TO TERMINATING OPERATIONS

Once the decision to terminate an operation has been made, the steps involved are straightforward. Similar to taking inventory, termination is a process that can be systematized, and if all steps are followed, then desired results can be achieved.

> ### STEPS TO FOLLOW
>
> 1. Consider the effects.
> 2. Verify the financials:
>   * fixed assets, accounts receivable, other assets;
>   * liabilities, accounts payable, contractual liabilities and leases;
>   * current revenues and expenses.
> 3. Estimate the costs of terminating operations.
> 4. Consider decisions about personnel:
>   * reutilization;
>   * early retirement and voluntary separation;
>   * layoffs and outplacement — government notice regulations.

5. Review reducing operations:
  * reducing the work week;
  * temporary closings.
6. Consider subcontracting business.
7. Determine the value to be recovered from termination.

Consider the Effects

Whether the company has decided to terminate all or just certain segments of the business, the process is the same. The first step is to meet with the senior managers of the firm and inform them of the decision. Listen to the company's managers. Be certain you understand all the possible effects and repercussions that terminating the operation will have on the company's remaining business.

Terminating operations has internal effects on the company as well as external effects based upon the perception that outsiders (vendors, customers, and the media) will have after hearing the news.

Internal Effects

The internal effects are the results when viewed by the firm's employees and operational management. Internal concerns include: diminished employee morale, the unavailability of terminated resources (personnel, production, parts inventory, etc.), and the under-utilization of vacant real estate. Internal effects can also be beneficial and include the additional cash flow and capital that are potentially available for other more deserving areas of the business.

External Effects

The external effects of terminating operations are the results in the marketplace when viewed from the perspective of the firm's customers, vendors, and competitors. These effects can include: lost revenues, reduced product offerings, continuing financial obligations, employee severance costs, contractual obligations, inability to hold market position, and a possible loss of formerly achieved strategic objectives (market share, key accounts, territory, etc.)

Public Relations

Don't ignore the public relations (PR) factor. The image of how the termination is presented to those outside the company can greatly alter its impact upon the remainder of the business.

The effect on PR of terminating parts of the business can be positive, negative, or benign. Properly handled, the external view of the company might even be that management is exercising sound business judgement.

At the worst, you want the view to be one of sympathy, with customers and vendors saying, "It's the economy" or "It's happening to everyone." What you want to avoid is projecting the image that the company is failing.

Remember that no one likes to hear bad news as a surprise. At the proper time, inform the company's customers, vendors, and employees about the company's plans for terminating operations. No one keeps bad news secret. Assume that if you tell one vendor or one customer, that the information will be known by all vendors and customers within a few days.

Work with the company's managers to prepare a short white paper listing commonly asked questions and answers (Q&A) about the termination. Why is the company terminating the operation? When will it be effective? What does it mean to customers with back orders? Where should customers go for service? Spare parts? What will happen to the employees? When will suppliers be paid?

Make the Q&A simple and succinct (i.e., try to tell a story that a reasonable businessperson would believe). Put a contact name and telephone number on the Q&A to answer any additional questions.

Provide the receptionist and managers with the Q&A. Post additional copies of the Q&A in places where most employees will have the opportunity to read it during the first day that it is posted. Send copies to other offices. The easiest way to avoid rumours is to answer the questions before the rumours start.

Media Attention

Be prepared for the media. Designate one person in the firm as the press contact and give the receptionist their home phone number. The press may not come, it depends how noteworthy the news is and what else happened that week. Don't go looking for media attention, but if the media knocks on your door, don't be caught napping.

The easiest way to dispel rumours is to promote your own version of the truth. If the press ask questions, don't be afraid to give them (or send via fax) a copy of the Q&A, or prepare a special Q&A for the press.

Avoid the consequences of negative publicity. These can include: customers canceling orders, leaving the company with additional inventory, and vendors demanding immediate payment or failing to make deliveries.

Write a personalized letter to each vendor and customer who is affected. The letter should explain the reasons for the closing, the effective date, and what it will mean to the company's business relationship with them.

Verifying the Financials

An important step in the process of terminating or reducing an operation is to **quantify** and to **verify** the financials associated with the subject business. The required financials include: lists of fixed assets, accounts receivable, other assets, accounts payable, other liabilities, current revenues and expenses, the expected costs of terminating or reducing operations and the value to be recovered from the operation.

Existing financials can be useful as a guide, when trying to rescue a business. However, remember the rule not to rely upon financials that were generated without your direct supervision. The assumptions that were made on the valuations of fixed assets, receivables, and inventory for taxes or financial statements are not very useful to the manager overseeing a turnaround.

Fixed Assets

Obtain or create a detailed and complete list of the fixed assets of the business to be terminated. **Detailed** means including serial numbers, manufacturers, and model numbers of fixed assets, where available. **Complete** means that all items that could be considered assets should be included.

We have seen a Cadillac listed on the balance sheet at $6,000 because that was the balance remaining on the bank loan used to purchase the car. The same vehicle was later appraised for $10,000. We have also seen electronics shops with $50,000 of very marketable tools and equipment written off as improvements to real estate with no recoverable value.

WARNING

Do not rely upon the list of fixed assets unless the inventory was recently performed and you personally trust the competency and the loyalty of the managers who supervised the physical inventory.

The fact that an inventory, or any financial report, was performed under the supervision of a chartered accounting firm is no guarantee that the details are accurate. It means that the generally accepted accounting principles were supposed to have been followed, but most CAs would agree that there is no substitute for a fresh and complete physical inventory of all assets.

Accounts Receivable

Create a complete list of **all** accounts receivable (AR). Pay particular attention to accounts that were "written off" or marked uncollectible during the past 12 months. The AR documents should include the credit information on each customer that has done business with the company during the past year, copies of all outstanding invoices, an aging report for each customer, and a summary report for all customers. See the chapter on *Managing Receivables* for a complete discussion on handling and collecting receivables.

Other Assets

Do not neglect the search for other assets after locating all of those detailed on the balance sheet. The sale of assets no longer essential to the business of the company can be an important source of cash.

Richard Miller, former CEO of Wang Laboratories Inc., spent three years uncovering and selling nonstrategic assets to raise money to keep the company alive. After he took the helm in 1989, Miller sold nonstrategic assets and recouped more than $300 million to keep Wang out of bankruptcy court. Although his efforts could not stem the tide and the company eventually filed for reorganization in bankruptcy in late 1992, Mr. Miller had purchased three years of breathing room by the sale of assets unessential to the core business.[2]

Don't forget about other assets: What about computer or office equipment in the personal possession of current or past employees? Spare parts and equipment at customer sites? Security deposits on utilities? Company-owned radios and cellular telephones? Deposits for mailings at the post office and mailing houses? Co-op advertising and promotional credits? Old bank accounts? Refunds for airline tickets? Insurance settlements? Advance deposits for trade shows and conferences?

Liabilities

The cardinal rule to remember when considering liabilities is that most can be renegotiated. Liabilities that are of concern when terminating the business or reducing operations are: accounts payable, contractual liabilities, payroll-related liabilities, and current expenses.

Accounts Payable

Payables are bills the company needs to pay or renegotiate. When terminating or selling operations, don't make the mistake of overstating or understating the accounts payable. Read carefully the chapter entitled *Managing Payables* for instructions on how to verify payables and negotiate with vendors.

Contractual Liabilities

Contractual liabilities can include leases, loan agreements, uniform delivery and laundry contracts, janitorial contracts, waste removal contracts, maintenance contracts, telephone answering services, security services, and blanket purchase orders. Although some of these businesses will initiate litigation to recover the damages incurred in early terminations of contracts, most are reasonable and will negotiate.

Leases

Leases can be grouped into three basic categories: vehicle, equipment, and real estate. You must also consider whether the lease is an obligation of the corporation, or if an officer or employee cosigned (personally guaranteed or accepted joint responsibility) for the obligation.

The terms and conditions of leases are often the easiest liabilities to renegotiate for a business that is terminating operations. Evaluate your position and use your leverage when negotiating. Vehicle and equipment leases can be sold, renegotiated, or terminated. Leases for real estate are special cases and it is wise to seek the assistance of a trained professional when renegotiating these types of agreements. For a complete discussion on leases for real estate, see the chapter on *Real Estate*.

An experienced lawyer should review each of the company's leases and identify the responsible parties and the order and trigger for each obligation. Analysis of obligations and guarantees relating to leases will also be necessary to evaluate the results of a bankruptcy filing or insolvency proceeding.

For a complete discussion on leases including vehicle, equipment, and property leases see the section on "Leases" in the chapter on *Managing Payables*.

Current Revenues

In terminating an operation, make a strong effort to collect on all current revenues. These revenues may be an important (and possibly critical) source of cash during the last few weeks, or months, of operations.

If customers have orders pending that have not been filled and the items are in inventory, then ship today. Do not delay. If orders are pending that are beyond the company's current capabilities or are not scheduled for delivery until too far into the future, then consider "selling" the order to a competitor or a colleague in exchange for a commission on the sale. Depending on the business, the company may not even have to inform the customer. Where it is necessary to inform the customer, an introduction from you may be all that is necessary to pave the way to a sale and earn your company a commission.

Current Expenses

Once the decision has been made to terminate operations, you must begin trimming expenses everywhere. All purchases above a preset limit **must** be approved by one designated person. Don't let anyone convince you that the company can't operate with such severe constrictions. In 1984, the brokerage giant Merrill Lynch had such a poor year that assistant vice presidents were limited in spending authority to less than $50! You must rapidly impose direct control on all expenses. Look everywhere to reduce overhead and expenses.

Informing the staff that the company will be terminating operations is not sufficient to control expenditures. Employees will act as they have been trained.

Senior management's view is that the office will be closing in 30 days and any surplus office supplies will be wasted. The office manager's view is that if the supply room is low on inventory, then they need to reorder. The office manager doesn't think about what will happen at the end of next month — it's not their job.

Reduce the number of outside telephone lines immediately. The company won't need any lines in two months' time, and at an average cost of $150 to $200 per line, per month, telecommunications can be a significant part of fixed overhead. The company could probably eliminate one-third of its telephone lines with little impact on the business.

Cancel all employee travel, conventions, exhibitions, car and gasoline allowances, and restrict the use of the corporate travel agency. Recall all but the absolutely necessary company charge cards and cancel all remaining charge account privileges (gas stations, office supplies, etc.). Cancel all orders for goods that have not been received. Reduce or eliminate all scheduled services such as pest control, janitorial, and landscaping.

Appoint one of your trusted lieutenants as the absolute master of the warehouse, loading dock, and shipping dock. All shipments arriving from vendors, unless they contain products that have already been sold to a customer, should be **refused** at the loading dock. Acceptance of new shipments will only increase the company's current liabilities.

Review the sections on Reducing Overhead for a more complete discussion of the types of expenses that can be reduced or eliminated.

DETERMINING THE COSTS OF TERMINATING OPERATIONS

There is an old maxim that "It takes money to make money." This maxim should be rewritten for a business discontinuing an operation as, "It can take money to stop losing money." There are many costs directly attributable to the termination of a business. These costs can include: severance and vacation payroll, advertising to sell inventory, security costs (locksmiths, night watch persons, etc.), temporary storage facilities for corporate records and inventory, professional fees (legal, accounting, and consulting), outplacement fees, and penalties imposed for the early cancellation of leases and contracts (use worst-case assumptions).

Because of the company's plans, vendors will probably not extend credit or accept cheques that haven't been certified and many expenses will need to be paid in cash. Estimate the costs associated with terminating an operation and prepare for them.

Payroll, Severance, Benefits, and Final Reimbursable Expenses

Prepare a very liberal forecast of the costs of terminating employees. There are four areas of costs to be concerned about: payroll, severance, benefits, and final reimbursable expenses.

Payroll   Forecast payroll costs from now until the effective date of the employees' departure or the company's termination of operations. Include in the forecast any commissions earned and owed.

Severance   Some employees may be entitled to severance pay if required by company policy, union contract, or provincial law. The company may have some flexibility with the timing and distribution of these payments, lump-sum vs. payments over time. Be prepared that employees, upon hearing the news or rumour of a closing, may announce immediate retirement and be entitled to additional severance pay.

If the company can afford to do so, it may opt to offer employees additional severance based on the length of their employment. Although this can be expensive, the company can reap benefits from its sensitivity to the plight of discharged employees. **The more humane the treatment of those laid off, the less traumatic and harmful the effect will be upon the remaining employees.**

Benefits   While the company may reduce some optional benefits, it may not cut out statutory benefits until the end of operations.

All employees must receive proper legal notice and termination and holiday pay as specified by federal and provincial labour and termination laws.

Final Expenses   Although the company is terminating operations, they may still owe additional benefits including accrued tuition reimbursement, vacation pay, and sick pay. Issue a written policy to all employees that any requests for reimbursable expenses, travel, and entertainment must be received by the company within five business days. Use the memo to restate the company policy regarding receipts and proof of expenditures.

DECISIONS ABOUT PERSONNEL

Although the manager is advised to read the chapter on *Personnel* in this book which covers the issues of personnel decisions in a troubled business thoroughly, the following are a few key rules that will help you.

A GUIDE TO PERSONNEL DECISIONS
FOR THE TROUBLED BUSINESS

1. Establish personnel objectives (reduce staff, reduce costs, or both).
2. Consider all the alternatives to layoffs to meet your objectives:
   - reduced working hours;
   - salary reductions;
   - reutilization or transfer of employees;
   - loaning or sharing of employees;
   - early retirement;
   - voluntary separation;
   - temporary furloughs;
   - temporary closings of operations.
3. Once the decisions have been made, be expeditious and firm in decisions to retain or terminate employees.
4. Where possible, always try outplacement of discharged personnel.

Employee Layoffs   Where redundancy is present, or employees can be readily replaced, companies may choose to lay off portions of their staff. Although the economic cost can be minimal, the emotional cost of terminating employees can be significant.

Before making any decisions to lay off employees, first examine methods for reducing costs and increasing revenues. The following are a few alternatives to employee layoffs which are discussed fully in the chapter on *Personnel.*

Reducing the Work Week/Work Day   Reducing the number of hours worked each week as an alternative to employee layoffs has been used as a method of reducing payroll costs by many Fortune 100 firms.

Salary Reductions   Some firms have opted to reduce salaries in particular jobs or across the entire company as a method of reducing payroll while avoiding terminating employees.

Reutilization   This may be done in the form of demotions, downgrades, or transfers to other jobs. Any employees that you want to use in other areas of the company or transfer to other offices should be informed immediately that a position is available, and they only have a few days in which to make a decision.

Loaning or Sharing an Employee   An alternative to using the employee within the company is to place the employee with a customer or vendor on a temporary basis. This has been successfully done with technicians, customer service, and training personnel, who can be "loaned" or "rented" to customers or vendors for extended periods.

Early Retirement and Voluntary Separation   Many companies who have been reluctant to lay off staff have offered early retirement to their employees. Called "voluntary separation," these packages can be combined with outplacement assistance to find the "retirees" new employment.

Temporary Furloughs and Temporary Closings   Temporary furloughs for part of the workforce can include forced vacations or unpaid leaves of absence.

Outplacement   To maintain company morale among those not laid off, many firms provide outplacement counseling for their laid off employees.

REDUCING OPERATIONS

An alternative to terminating operations is to scale back and reduce production expenses that are necessary for, but separate from, the company's primary business. For some firms this can be done by subcontracting (also called "farming-out" or "outsourcing") or by reducing operational expenses.

There are many ways to trim operational expenses including reducing the hours worked each week, temporarily closing facilities, laying off employees, moving to smaller facilities, subcontracting business, and selling subsidiary nonessential operations. Reducing production capacity is sometimes called "downsizing," though new corporate missionaries are now calling it "rightsizing."

Subcontracting Business

Subcontracting operations can reduce production costs and relieve a company of the problems associated with an uneven or cyclical flow of orders. It can also allow a company to focus its attention on its core business. The company may be able to recover some of the working capital invested in the operation by selling the excess equipment, inventory, and facilities and subcontracting the business involved.

A business can subcontract an operation to reduce costs and sometimes also recover value for the capital invested in the operation. A vending machine distribution business had constructed and was staffing an electronics repair shop with five employees, $50,000 of sophisticated test equipment, and $75,000 of parts. The company had witnessed a reduction in the volume of repair orders and found that the costs of operating the repair facility no longer justified the expense.

The company subcontracted with an independent electronics shop to repair its products at a lower cost. The subcontractor agreed to purchase the firm's test equipment and spare parts. This is an example of a win-win situation for both businesses.

Sometimes the idea to subcontract comes from a desire to concentrate the firms resources on its primary business. Drake Beam Morin, Inc. (DBM), one of North America's largest outplacement consulting firms, had grown quickly and found itself with high costs and management problems in the internal operation that produced manuals and printed materials for their clients. DBM subcontracted the printing services resulting in lower costs and more time to focus on their primary business.[3]

When subcontracting achieves lower costs and employees that would have been laid off are hired by the subcontractor, then the contractor, the management, and the employees are all winners. John Fluke Mfg. Co. was able to achieve this type of win-win-win victory. The company, which is synonymous in the engineering world with quality hand-held meters, had grown steadily since its inception in 1948, and by 1992 an entire division was devoted to printing operations.

As part of a restructuring and cost reduction program, Fluke terminated its printing operation and contracted with a local firm to provide these services. Fluke was also able to "outplace" (find jobs for) six of its employees scheduled for layoffs.[4] As a result, Fluke reduced costs, a subcontractor got employees who already knew the business, and there was little negative effect on company morale because of the outplacement.

Germinating Subcontractors

Sometimes you can "germinate" a small business to serve the company's needs and simultaneously reduce costs. Take the example of the automobile dealership which needed a paint and body shop for repairs. During the last few years, the company observed that the used vehicles it received were in better condition and only occasionally needed body work. The company could no longer justify maintaining a repair shop.

The dealership's owner helped a group of employees to establish an independent paint and body shop. He sold them the tools and equipment from his shop on favourable terms and guaranteed them 100% of the dealership's repair business.

The dealership had achieved a win-win-win situation. It had reduced its costs, recovered good value for the assets, and outplaced a group of employees.

Temporary Closings

Where the costs of operations can be immediately reduced by a temporary closing of facilities, the manager of a troubled firm should carefully evaluate the option. This technique has primarily been used by large firms, but small- and medium-sized firms may also find value in closing offices and facilities for several weeks during holiday or slow seasons.

Determining Value to be Recovered from Termination

W A R N I N G

Once the company has announced layoffs, or the termination of an operation, it needs to monitor closely the warehouse and all facilities. Inventory, tools, and supplies have a way of disappearing under unusual circumstances following the notice of a facility closing. Don't hesitate to change the locks, hire security guards, and impose whatever new controls are needed to preserve and protect the company's remaining assets.

Operations that are terminated or reduced usually have surplus assets which can be sold. Do it today. Tomorrow the items will be worth less and the storage will be an additional cost. You can sell as surplus just about anything the company has: used office supplies, office furniture, fixtures, storage racks, packing and mailing supplies, cleaning supplies, inventory, spare parts, manuals, and computer software.

Make a list of all surplus assets and put approximate resale values on the items. Don't hold out on yourself. Why do you need three photocopy machines when you have reduced your staff to fifteen employees? Sell it! Sell anything you can; the cash value you recover is far more valuable today than the asset will be tomorrow.

NOTES

[1]A personal anecdote on the illusory "image of success" involves two firms, both of which appeared to be very successful: Businessland, Inc. and Integrated Resources, Inc. While managing a small computer company, we proposed to sell a system to Integrated. Several weeks later, they called and said that, although we had the best product, because of concerns about the "future financial viability" of our company they had chosen Businessland. Within a year, history delivered a pyrrhic victory. Integrated filed for bankruptcy protection and Businessland was insolvent. We then realized that we were more financially stable and viable than either of those two "images of success."

[2]*United Press International*, October 24, 1989, "Wang to sell $212 million in assets," and *The New York Times*, August 19, 1992, p.D-1, "Wang files for bankruptcy...."

[3]*Business Wire, Inc.*, February 12, 1992, "IMT to manage client manuals for Drake Beam Morin."

[4]*The Seattle Times*, November 20, 1992, p.D-9, "Fluke to restructure operations," Karen Alexander.

CHAPTER 8

REAL ESTATE

THE LARGEST EXPENSE the firm or business has next to payroll is the cost of facilities. This consists of two components: the rent or mortgage payment, and the regular operating expenses of property taxes, insurance, utilities, maintenance, common area charges, cleaning, security, and landscaping.

THE GOOD NEWS

The good news is that as the result of the massive overbuilding of the commercial and industrial real estate markets of the late 1980s, there is excess supply in nearly every Canadian market. Vacancy rates range from 27% in Toronto office space to 20% in Montreal and 17% in Vancouver.

As a result, it is strictly a buyer's/renter's market. The negotiating power is in your hands. In most cases landlords will accept any reasonable restructuring or forbearance proposals. Canada is filled with retailers paying no rent for a year and postponing payments until the end of the lease or extending it a year. Businesses in office towers are regularly getting lower rents, postponements, and forbearance agreements, or with the aid of the landlord, they are moving to less space at lower cost in the same building.

Industrial space is being converted to small business incubators, low-cost housing for the homeless, or flea markets. Even Revenue

Canada does not want industrial buildings. From Halifax to Vancouver, tens of millions of square feet of space sit vacant.

This is the best time in nearly 15 years to renegotiate space-related overheads. Landlords would rather have a building that appears filled with tenants paying some rent, than one sitting vacant, making it unattractive to other tenants.

During their growth and expansion mode, most businesses took at least 20% extra space as a contingency allowance. Just as many firms became overstaffed, most become "overspaced" as well.

Few businesses audit their overall space costs. Retailers rarely check to see if mall owners are overcharging on common area costs and taxes. The bad news is that most are.

ATTACKING THE COSTS

Attacking the cost of real estate is critical to any survival plan and the lessons learned should be remembered during the resurrection phase. Any would-be white knight investor, new lender or purchaser will look at real estate costs at the very beginning of their assessment. Getting these costs under control and in line is essential early in the survival plan to establish credibility. Creditors will view your downsizing of space as a tangible start in your efforts to accumulate and conserve cash to pay their bills or bank loans.

There are a number of alternative ways of reducing the cost of real estate. These methods include: closing locations, consolidating operations, negotiating a reduction of rent or mortgage payments, moving to a new location, or subletting some of your space.

METHODS TO REDUCE RENT OR MORTGAGE PAYMENTS

- Close locations
- Consolidate operations
- Negotiate a reduction or forbearance on current payments
- Renegotiate the terms and conditions of the lease
  - early termination
  - early renewal or extension
- Move to a new location
- Sublet some of your space
- Establish a cooperative sharing your space.

Closing Locations

When contemplating the closing of a location or facility, answer the following questions: Do you really need each of your locations? Does the revenue generated from the location justify the cost of operating it? Do customers visit your office? Would customers be unwilling to travel to another of your locations?

As an alternative, could your employees travel to the customers' locations? Are you maintaining the location for image, for future business, or for additional revenue to the bottom line this year? How much business would you lose if you closed the office? Could you use alternate facilities to perform the same or similar operations at a lower cost? What additional costs would the company incur by operating the business from an alternative location? With the movement today to the telecommuting worker and the proliferation of fax machines, modems, and mobile sales forces, the fixed-office headquarters is obsolescent.

One computer sales firm, fighting for survival in a cost-competitive market, reduced its regional offices in 10 cities from 20,000 sq. ft. to 2,000 with clerical staff, accounting, and a district sales manager. All full-time sales staff were given a suitcase containing a notebook computer, mini-fax, and cellular phone. They all work out of their cars and homes and only attend sales meetings at the office. Mail is directed to their homes. Office costs and related overheads have declined by nearly 60%, despite the expenditure on the new computer hardware for the workers.

Clearly the large, fixed, city-centre office is a phenomenon of the 1980s not the 1990s. In their movement toward the vertical (hollow) organization, many companies have downsized middle management by as much as 25%. The 75% organization is more cost efficient, competitive, and productive.

Most importantly it uses less space, less clerical overhead, and less cash.

Moving While Under the Gun

The troubled firm doesn't usually want to advertise a move. Letting the public know you are moving can be like ringing the alarm bell for creditors.

Although secrecy is not always necessary when planning a move, it can be advantageous in some situations.

We have all heard the stories and jokes about "Midnight Movers," with companies moving their goods at three o'clock in the morning to avoid landlords. This is neither ethical nor beneficial in the long term.

In some situations and for strategic negotiating reasons, some companies have moved out secretly to avoid publicity and to present a competitor, regulator, or landlord with a fait accompli.

If the lease is not guaranteed by an individual, the company may consider this option. Some national moving companies have expertise in this area and will charge a premium to do it. They will wish to be paid in cash or certified cheque.

When to Consolidate Operations

Consolidating operations into one location can often benefit the company by reducing the real estate costs of separate operations and by eliminating any resulting overlaps in resources (human, equipment, vehicles, inventory, and supplies, taxes and overheads).

Can you consolidate some of the company's operations into other space already occupied by your company? Do you need to lease new space and consolidate multiple operations into one location? Could you share space with another company?

An example where consolidation of discrete operations reduced costs was an electronics manufacturer that maintained separate sales and service facilities.

The sales office, located in a high-priced corporate office park, was used by its sales staff to make telephone calls, to prepare for meetings, and to store product samples and literature. The office space when originally leased was furnished nicely to project a professional image to the firm's customers. However, the company had discovered that customers rarely visited the sales office and 90% of all sales were made by salespersons visiting the customer.

The service facility included under-utilized space and was located in a mixed-usage light industrial park adjacent to a highway. The company renegotiated its lease on the service facility and agreed to renew the lease for an additional five years, in exchange for the landlord building a sales office (at no out-of-pocket cost to the company) in the front of the service facility.

The company moved the sales offices into the service facility and significantly reduced its monthly real estate costs. The company also realized several additional benefits. The new facility was more conveniently located to the highway and gave the salespersons quicker access to customers. The company could now place the product samples and literature in the existing stockroom, with the proper inventory control procedures necessary to maintain adequate stocks. The company also realized cost savings by reducing the number of telephone lines required; laying off one receptionist and one secretary; and eliminating one fax machine, one photocopy machine, and one postage meter. There were also savings in taxes, maintenance, and stationary.

Many noncompeting professionals have consolidated offices. Lawyers, accountants, consultants, financial planners, insurance agents, and engineers regularly consolidate in an office building sharing common reception, board rooms, fax machines, photocopiers, clerical staff, and telephone systems. The net result is that the facility gives the impression of large space and a prime location, but with shared common costs based on utilization, everyone pays less than if they were on their own.

We also see retailers placing boutiques within existing stores — "a shop in a shop" — to reduce costs and capitalize on traffic. Consolidating and closing for retailers or consumer service businesses is particularly conspicuous. When a retailer with six stores reduces his size to three everyone notices, including customers and creditors.

We have regularly counseled retailers that store consolidation in the 1990s is less damaging than it was five years ago. Consolidate the excess or unsalable inventory into a warehouse location and use the warehouse as a clearance centre. You can normally get one month's lease to conduct the sale and it keeps the store image intact. It frees up all your own warehouse space and cleans out your store space quickly, without damaging the store image of your remaining outlets.

It is easier to consolidate for retailers if they have common landlords who appreciate the need to survive. This means keeping the good stores open and paying the landlord rent while the nonperformers are closed.

Many retailers are consolidating by establishing one superstore or warehouse branch instead of a dozen small locations. For retailers in difficulty, consolidation is both important as well as potentially dangerous. It signals to suppliers and competitors that there are difficulties, but in most situations it becomes a basic survival option.

Analyze the operations of each location, applying full corporate overheads to determine if there is a positive cash flow from operations. If the store generates a negative cash flow and there is no strategic reason such as profile to keep it open, then the location must be closed. It will save direct rental costs plus costs of supervision and inventory.

Long drawn-out closing sales are not the answer. Our retail research shows that the two best options are to transfer inventory to other locations to reduce mark downs, or to conduct a one-week blow-out sale to grab as much cash as possible. Both minimize system damage by reducing the negative visibility of a close-out sale.

When to Separate Operations

Sometimes the existing consolidation can result in higher real estate costs than operating the business from separate locations. In these situations the company can reap a cost savings by separating the operations into different locations.

Separation is most efficient where operations requiring significant amounts of low-cost space (warehouses and manufacturing facilities) are combined with retail or front office operations which require small quantities of expensive frontage or space.

An example of a business which had entered a troubled period because of the high cost of maintaining consolidated facilities was a dry-cleaning business located in Toronto. The family-owned firm operated a processing facility at its main midtown location and maintained five satellite drop-off locations in Toronto. The company was operating at full capacity but losing money every month. These losses were a result of the high fixed costs of paying rent for their main location. They were operating the processing plant in a location where they were paying a high rent for retail frontage space.

Faced with imminent eviction for three months' past-due rent on their main location, the company was forced to move. Because of the strong resistance of dry-cleaning customers to walk two blocks to a new location, the company feared losing its most valuable asset — its customers. All of the nearby alternative locations were either too expensive or not suitable for combined use as a retail location and processing facility.

A consultant examining the troubles of the business recommended that the firm separate the processing facility from the retail operation. The consultant suggested they lease a small retail space across the street from the current location as a new drop-off location, thereby maintaining a "hold" on their current customers. The company located a dry-cleaning plant in Brampton which had excess capacity and was willing to lease its plant and machinery to the company every night from 6 p.m. to 6 a.m.

The result was that the company, by separating operations, was able to reduce its costs without losing any customers.

Another illustration is a Toronto-based women's clothing manufacturer which maintained a New York City showroom, combined with a small warehouse, totaling 10,000 sq. ft. in an expensive building frequented by the buyers for major retail stores.

The company needed more local warehouse space but couldn't afford the expense. The cost of maintaining the present warehouse was already too high and the company was in a period of financial difficulty. After considering its options, the company moved its showroom to a smaller 3,000 sq. ft. space on a more desirable floor in the same building and moved its warehouse to a 12,000 sq. ft. space in an industrial building located on a nearby side street.

The result was that the company gained a better showroom and a larger warehouse at a total cost of less than half of the original combined facility.

Negotiating a Reduction in or Forbearance on Current Payments

Why is it often possible to renegotiate leases and mortgages? Because most lenders and lessors are reasonable and want your company to remain financially strong enough to continue as their customer.

Use Your Negotiating Skills   Most business persons sign a lease or mortgage and assume that the only opportunity for them to change the terms and conditions is prior to the signing or upon renewal. **This is a myth.** The terms and conditions of property leases and mortgages, although fixed in writing as legal documents, are not carved in stone and can often be renegotiated to your company's benefit. The more troubled your business is, the greater likelihood you have of renegotiating the original terms and conditions.

> ### R E M I N D E R
> The cardinal rule of the troubled firm is: if those you do business with (customers, vendors, banks, and lessors) will benefit more by your staying in business than by your closing, then you have leverage with which to negotiate and should treat everything as negotiable.

Renegotiating the Terms and Conditions of the Lease

You can renegotiate a lease in any type of real estate market. In a market sparse with new tenants, the property owner will be very flexible to avoid having a vacant property. In a market flush with new prospective tenants, the property owner will be likely to look favourably upon an early termination of the lease where there exists the opportunity to gain a new tenant at a higher rent.

Start off by examining the costs of your leases. At what cost can you afford to remain in your present location? Is there enough time remaining on the lease for you to pay less rent now, during the troubled period, and more rent at the end of the lease? Is the lease renewable at the end of the year? You may be able to use an early renewal as an incentive for the landlord to agree to terms more favourable to the present financial condition of your business.

Is it simply a question of a few months of not paying rent to allow the company to "stay alive" for the next year? Ask the lessor to agree to grant you a forbearance for the next three months of rent and then stretch the payments for past-due rent over the next three years.

Do you owe three months' back rent? Then include the three months owed (called a "deficiency") in your negotiations. As long as you include the past-due amounts in your negotiations, then the lessor believes they have some hope of recovery. You don't need to pay the past-due rent, just include it in discussions.

Always keep the hope of future prosperity alive in negotiations. If you don't keep a positive outlook and keep hope alive, no one else will. Be realistic, but remain optimistic about the prospects for the future, if only the landlord would grant you these small favours.

Landlords in general are a reasonable lot. If you tell them in advance of your difficulties and communicate openly, forbearance is far more likely.

Some landlords may offer to allow you to move to less attractive space in the same building or mall. You are still at the same address, so on the surface nothing has changed.

Being Paid to Terminate a Lease

Even when you are several months behind in your rent payments there are possibilities for terminating leases to your company's advantage. You may be surprised that a landlord can be convinced to pay your company (yes, the landlord will pay you!) to terminate a lease early where they can move in a new tenant at a higher rent.

When you agree to terminate a lease or to extend its term, whatever be the lessor's desire, you are giving the lessor something they want and you will discover that terms can be changed, past-due rent put aside, eviction proceedings halted, and monthly rental payments renegotiated.

Avoiding Defaulting on Mortgages

Contrary to the gothic horror stories, lenders don't usually want you to default on a mortgage, which would result in their foreclosing on the property. Lenders are not in the business of managing real estate. They are in the business of lending money for a secured interest in real property and receiving the money back in instalments with interest.

Try not to wait until the mortgage holder has initiated foreclosure proceedings to communicate your desire to negotiate. Even if you can't make a full payment, don't despair, most mortgage lenders only want to see some regular payment (they call it "debt service"), even if the payment is only for half the amount due.

What Do Lenders Want?

What do lenders want? They want to see some debt service and they want to know that the underlying property is being maintained and will not lose its value. The lender wants to know that the mortgagee is doing everything they can to make full payments or, in the alternative, to rent or sell the property with the proceeds being paid to the lender. They'll want the insurance on the property kept up to date to protect their mortgage interest.

What Should You Ask from Lenders?

Try asking the lender to agree to accept only the interest portion of the mortgage obligation, with a forbearance on the principal payments for the next six or 12 months. After the end of the period, agree to resume interest and principal payments and have the missing principal added to the original mortgage amount.

If you need a three-month deferral of mortgage payments, then ask the lender for a three-month forbearance and have the difference added to the original mortgage (i.e., extend the term of the mortgage a few months).

If you are moving and unable to make any significant payments to the lender, agree to list the property for sale or rental with a real estate agent. Ask the lender for a realtor they would recommend. Demonstrate to the lender that you are doing everything you can in good faith to "turn around" the situation to the lender's benefit.

METHODS OF REDUCING MORTGAGE PAYMENTS

- Payments of interest only, forbearance on principal
- Payment on a quarterly basis from a monthly
- Forbearance of three months' principal and interest
- Full forbearance and list property for rent or sale
- Rent property with direct assignment of rents to mortgage holder — forbearance on any deficiency
- Rent a portion of property with direct assignment of rents to the mortgage holder — forbearance on any deficiency
- Rescheduling of debt at new lower rates with a small penalty payment.

Seek Professional Assistance (Very Important)

Unless you are only asking for a few months' forbearance in payments when renegotiating a property lease or mortgage, it is strongly recommended that you seek the assistance of a trained professional. Ask your colleagues to recommend real estate professionals or lawyers with specialties in real estate who can assist you in renegotiating leases and mortgages. Only a professional will know what your rights are and how to protect your company from harm while renegotiating and legally confirm these types of arrangements so they will be durable for the future.

> ## W A R N I N G
>
> Whatever arrangement you make, be certain that the changes and conditions are agreed to in writing, so you are not suddenly faced with an eviction or foreclosure proceeding because the lessor or mortgage holder changed their mind. Retailers have less flexibility and the landlords may act more quickly to close the business.

Moving to a New Location

You may evaluate your current location and decide that there is either no way to cost-effectively utilize the property, or the landlord will not negotiate a satisfactory reduction in rent. Then MOVE! Don't delay and don't wait until the landlord sends you an eviction notice. Your objective is to locate your company where you can make a profit.

Don't Worry about Breaking Leases

Although the landlord can use the legal system to seek a judgement against your company for rent past due and can include claims for damages for early termination of the lease, don't lose any sleep over their waving of spears. Most landlords' barks are far worse than their bite. They may threaten litigation but rarely take the recourse except for eviction proceedings. Primarily, they want tenants who pay the rent on time, do not complain, and who lease in an orderly manner.

Although landlords will threaten to change the locks on the doors and to refuse you permission to move out, these are not usually powers that are within their legal rights. Refusing to permit your company to move or holding your property can subject a landlord to significant liability for the loss to your business and possible criminal charges for "conversion," the legal term for taking your property and treating it as their own.

Landlords know that courts do not view litigation for damages based on early termination of leases, particularly those where the tenant has already vacated the space, as high priority cases. These cases languish in the court dockets for years. A reasonable real estate lawyer can raise defenses on your behalf and use the state rules of civil procedure to delay the landlord's day in court for at least a year, and possibly as long as three years. The landlord must act to mitigate his damages by trying to rent the space and reduce his losses.

Every month that goes by is another month that you can work on rebuilding your business, and the landlord must continue paying his lawyer to pursue a legal remedy. Even when the landlord gets to court, if you have defenses such as a leaky roof, or insufficient heating or air-conditioning, you may have offsets against the amount you owe the landlord. Furthermore, at any time prior to judgement being issued, you can instruct your counsel to negotiate an out-of-court settlement with the landlord.

In summary, if you have to break a lease because you have no alternative, then do it! Try to negotiate, but if the results are not sufficient to keep the company alive, then walk. Walk away quietly and discreetly, but walk away.

Where to Move

As a financially distressed company, don't look for a new long-term lease when moving. You may not find the optimal space. Instead, find space that works for you. Do you need office space, a warehouse, or a manufacturing plant? Can you share space with another firm? Take a month-to-month rental if you must. It might cost a little more in the short term but gives you no fixed obligation.

Move to a property that works for you, not for your dreams of what might have been. It is better to move to a low-cost space for a year and then move to a more attractive space when you have completed your business recovery. Once you have moved, moving a second time will take considerably less effort.

How to Move

When moving under threat of eviction or other debtor-creditor related litigation, plan the move very carefully. Start cleaning up and packing as much as possible in advance, but do not give the appearance that you are packing.

Plan the move well and be certain you take **everything** with you when you leave. Once you have vacated the premises, expect that the landlord will change the locks or post a security guard within a few hours.

Dos and Don'ts of Moving

The following is a list of Dos and Don'ts for troubled companies planning a move, while under the gun of one or more creditors.

DOs

- Do advise your lawyer that you may need their services on the day of the move. This way you will have counsel available if the landlord denies your company access to the freight elevator or bars the doors.
- Do have cash available to take care of tips for elevator operators, local security guards, and porters.
- Do hire a moving company from the other side of town.
- Do prearrange for your telephone lines to be switched automatically to your new location.
- Do give the post office a letter in writing requesting them to hold all mail for the company, at the post office, for one week.
- Do change your bank accounts.

DON'Ts

- Don't advise the landlord that you will be moving.
- Don't advise your customers and vendors you will be moving. You'll have plenty of time to inform them later.
- Don't fill out a Change of Address card at the post office in advance.

If you own too much furniture or equipment for your new location then try to sell as much as you can. See Chapter 7 under *Terminating and Reducing Operations* for suggestions and a guide to disposing of excess of furniture and equipment. What you can't sell place in storage in one of the now commonplace rent-a-room storage facilities which can be leased for $25 to $50 per month.

SUBLETTING SOME OF YOUR SPACE

If it's not possible to move, or if the cost of relocating is too expensive, consider subletting or renting a portion of your space. If your lease does not permit you to sublet the space, do it anyway. As long as the landlord is receiving rent he is unlikely to be concerned about your subletting space.

Your ideal tenant is a company in a related or possibly complementary business. Avoid any company that competes with the business of your company. Try approaching some of your vendors or customers as potential subtenants. Consider what you have to offer a prospective tenant; he may be interested in sharing secretarial services, a receptionist, conference rooms, or warehouse space. If you have a sales office, consider approaching firms who don't have a sales office in your geographic area. Professional firms can usually share space with other noncompeting professional firms and they can even refer business.

You may not need a long formal agreement with your tenant, but you do want a security deposit. Don't accept a cheque from the tenant unless the cheque can be cashed before they move in. You don't want to find your company in the same position as your landlord.

Consider the type and quality of tenant you are looking for very carefully. Always check a tenant's past references. One horror story surrounds a subtenant who, after the first month, came in one weekend with a truck and cleaned out the original tenant's warehouse and was never heard from again. A well-chosen tenant can be a saviour. The wrong tenant can be the kiss of death. Make the sublet work for your company.

REDUCING OPERATING EXPENSES

As an alternative to moving or as a supplement to other cost reductions, most companies can reduce operating expenses associated with their real estate. You can reduce operating expenses by curtailing, economizing, or eliminating the following expenses: utilities, lights, security, landscaping, waste removal, and office cleaning.

To economize on HVAC (heating-ventilation-air-conditioning) install thermostats with timers in locked boxes. If you currently have maintenance contracts on the HVAC system, you may want to explore changing to a time and materials arrangement to reduce costs.

Designate an employee to make certain that all windows and doors are kept closed. Instruct employees to turn off power on all computers, copiers, and electrical equipment on evenings and weekends.

WARNING

Do not eliminate the property insurance. You may want to increase the deductibles, but keep the policy in force. See the section on "Reducing Insurance" in Chapter 4 for suggestions on how to reduce insurance costs, but do not eliminate coverage.

CHAPTER 9

PERSONNEL

THE FIRST PLACE that managers look to save money is payroll. Managers know if they fire employees they will reduce their labour costs. However, the problem of how to reduce costs without crippling the firm's productivity does not have such easy solutions. Although layoffs produce initial savings, the firms often pay a higher price in the costs of the trauma to the surviving business.[1] Our research shows that layoffs can result in loss of morale, declining customer service, less innovation, and loss of worker loyalty.

Many companies in Canada, the United States and Europe have used alternative personnel management strategies to successfully reduce labour costs and avoid involuntary layoffs. These alternatives include shortening the work week, reducing salaries, demoting or transferring employees, voluntary job sharing, limited duration furloughs, and early retirement incentives.

However, in two recent surveys, less than half of the firms that laid off employees in the last year considered all of the alternatives, first. There appear to be two reasons for this myopia: (1) managers may not be familiar with alternatives to layoffs, and (2) in times of crisis, managers are risk averse.

This section will discuss the various alternative employment strategies available to troubled companies, with examples of how other firms have successfully used them to reduce costs, while maintaining company morale and productivity and improving profitability. The traditional method of reducing labour costs, involuntary termination (firing) is treated with a step-by-step humanistic approach to managing the termination.

REDUCING BENEFITS

Sometimes, a company can be mistaken about the need to lay off employees to reduce costs. Employees' salaries and wages are only one element of the cost of labour. Employee benefits can represent an additional cost of 10% to 50% of a company's labour costs. By carefully evaluating, pruning, and trimming benefits, personnel costs can be reduced without the need to reduce staff.

The last W.M. Mercer and Associates 1994 Benefits Survey shows that 50% of employers are currently reviewing pension costs and 60% are reviewing benefits and salary costs.

This chapter explores the true costs of employee benefit packages and shows managers how to reduce these costs and instill in the employees an appreciation for the value of the benefits they are receiving.

Some Background on Benefits

Contrary to common belief, most businesses are under no legal requirement to provide any benefits other than unemployment and workers' compensation insurance. The primary reason for providing benefits is to be competitive in the marketplace for hiring and retaining the best employees. A good benefits package will attract good employees and is considered indicative of how a company's management feels about its workforce.

What Are the Company's Strategic Objectives?

Classical capitalists trying to maximize profits will pose the question, "What is the optimal level of benefits, that when provided to employees, will maximize their productivity?" Unfortunately, the answer is not as simple as the question.

A company has three constituencies: the employees, the shareholders, and the customers. Which constituency is the most important? Is the goal of the company to maximize return to the shareholders? Is the goal to provide the best quality service to its customers? Is the goal to compensate employees to keep them happy and productive? Balancing the demands of the various constituencies with the company's strategic objectives is a difficult task.

All of the goals mentioned may be necessary for a company to be successful, but the problem is that some goals can only be achieved at the cost of missing the mark on others. When making decisions on layoffs, alternatives to layoffs, and changes to employee benefits, management is defining the company's strategic objectives.

Gil Amelio, CEO of National Semiconductor Corp., who made the difficult decision to reduce benefits and lay off over 5,200 employees, said, "It's a terrible mistake if you only manage a company for one constituency. . .To keep people employed on a long-term basis, you have to do some painful things. Otherwise, there won't be any jobs at all."[2]

IBM Canada, Stelco, and General Motors Canada made similar pronouncements when they cut thousands of middle management jobs between 1990 and 1993. For example, the elimination of 10,000 jobs at IBM Canada appears, at least in the short term, to have saved the balance of the remaining positions, as the company returned to profitability in the first quarter of 1994.

Most troubled companies, when informed by experts that they need to reduce employee benefits, respond that they couldn't possibly do it without losing valuable employees. This is another myth that managers hide behind.

Although benefits are an important part of compensation, most employees would choose to keep their current job with reduced benefits instead of being unemployed. No benefits are inalienable rights and all are open for inspection.

Change Can Be Good

Before the turmoil of the last ten years of "downsizing" and "rightsizing" destroyed another illusion, many managers and employees acted under the impression that a good job, once found, was their privilege for life. If managed properly, correcting this falsehood can have very positive effects upon the surviving employees. Once employees are reminded that their job security rests with the profitability of the company, they begin to think differently.

A study by Arthur Anderson Consulting says of the survivors of corporate layoffs, "They begin to ask management difficult and direct questions: What are you doing to become more competitive? What are your plans for success? How do you plan to turn the company around?"[3]

We won't try to convince you that troubles are good for companies, but after reading this book you may agree that if the solutions to the troubles are well managed, the result can be a stronger company.

To review, there are three basic methodologies for reducing labour costs: reduce employee benefits, alternatives to layoffs, and terminating employees. The next few sections explore these methods and discuss how other firms use them to reduce costs.

METHODS TO REDUCE LABOUR COSTS
1. Reduce employee benefits.
2. Explore alternatives to layoffs.
3. Terminate employees.

Two Types of Employee Benefits

Benefits can be separated into two categories: the visible (direct) and the invisible (hidden) benefits.

Visible benefits are those "perks" and "fringes" that employees view as part of the "compensation package." These are the benefits that people consider when comparing your company to another job opportunity. These benefits can include health, life and disability insurance, sick leave, vacation days, company-provided automobiles or automobile allowances, subsidized day care, pension plans, profit-sharing plans, subsidized education and training programs, and other company services provided for the express benefit of the employees.

Invisible benefits are products and services that your company provides to your employees, knowingly or unknowingly, where the employee benefits. These benefits include the employees' personal use of company-provided telephones, mails, couriers, fax and photocopy machines. It also includes subsidized health-care provider services (company nurse and/or physician), subsidized food services, coffee and soda service, and travel discounts, etc. Employees are rarely aware of the full costs to the company of providing these invisible benefits and, as a result, are typically not appreciative of the value they receive.

REDUCING VISIBLE BENEFITS

Supplementary Health Care

All Canadian workers are covered by some form of mandated health care funded by payroll tax or premium payments. This system, cofunded by Ottawa, provides for public ward hospital stays and most doctor visit costs.

To augment this system, most employers provide supplemental health care including Blue Cross or some form of semiprivate or private hospital room insurance, as well as payments for dental, disability, prescription drugs, and life insurance. To this point, it is estimated by major benefit experts that about 60% of Canadian workers are covered by dental and prescription drug plans.

In addition, most jurisdictions have not to date taxed these benefits as part of compensation. Ontario and Quebec began to tax benefits at a reduced rate recently, and in 1994 the federal government extended this to include the $25,000 of life insurance not currently taxed.

Most of these extended benefit plans are partially funded by employees through copayments.

While statutory obligations on health care, U.I.C., C.P.P., and Workers' Compensation are mandatory and can only be reduced by laying off workers, the costs of most other plans can be reduced by placing them out to tender. This may result in reduce costs without reducing coverage.

Examine Your Current Coverage

In examining your current employee benefits package, ask yourself the following questions: Is the company's offering competitive in the industry or geographic area? Can the company afford to continue the benefits package in its current form? Would it be better to reduce benefits or lay off employees? Are the employees really benefiting from, and satisfied with, the current plan?

Although supplemental health insurance is one of the key benefits that employees consider before deciding on a job, don't be mistaken that your company is **required** to provide this perk. Many small and mid-size companies do not provide any supplemental insurance benefits, and recently some companies have either significantly reduced benefits or eliminated them altogether.

During a sharp downturn for the business there may be a need to eliminate employer contributions for some programs and require 100% copayments by the employees, but they will still realize savings because of the lower costs of group rates.

Satisfying Your Employees

If the intention is to keep the staff intact but still find a means to cut costs overall, then the starting point must be the effectiveness and comprehensiveness of the supplemental coverage.

Employees should be surveyed to determine the adequacy of coverage and the relevance of the plans. A young staff will make higher use of dental plans for their children and may have more maternity-related and pharmaceutical claims. Most employees would rather have a group plan at a lower cost, where they have to contribute copayment of 50% or more, than no plan at all.

REDUCING SUPPLEMENTAL HEALTH INSURANCE COSTS

- Increase employee contributions for premiums
- Eliminate or reduce employer payments of premiums for spousal and dependent coverage, dental, and disability and life insurance
- Change to a higher deductible
- Change type of policy (or insurance carrier)
- Adapt policy to meet changing demographics of workforce
- Increase waiting period for new hires to receive coverage.

Increase Employee Contributions

Typical employee contributions ("copayments") towards premiums for their supplemental insurance range from nothing to 50% of the premium cost, depending on the geographic area and the industry. In today's economy, a contribution of around 25% is competitive.

If providing a supplemental benefits package costs the company 15% of salary costs and the company institutes a 25% copayment plan, the result will be annual savings of at least 2.5% of payroll costs. In a firm with a $2.0 million annual payroll, savings of 2.5% are equivalent to $50,000 per year, which should easily represent two employees' jobs that were saved.

Reduce Employer Payments of Premiums for Spousal and Dependant Coverage, Dental Insurance, Disability and Life Insurance

Eliminating employer contributions for spousal and dependant coverage may seem drastic for the employer, who perceived themselves as benevolent parents to their employees, but the continued existence of the company may be at stake.

Canada Nut & Bolt, a medium-sized parts distributor, needed to cut costs to remain competitive. The troubled company had historically paid for all supplemental insurance for their employees and dependants. To reduce costs while avoiding layoffs, the company decided to purchase insurance coverage only for employees. Employees could continue coverage for their dependants, but the cost would be deducted from their paycheques. The results were cost savings and the departures of some employees, but the company was able to weather the storm.

Dental insurance is a great benefit for employees with children and older employees, but is of lesser importance to young and single or middle-aged employees. Although some forms of dental insurance can be obtained without a group, they are not as comprehensive and have lower maximum benefit limits. To reduce costs, have employees pay the majority (if not 100%) of the dental insurance premium through payroll deduction, and allow them to choose whether they want to be covered.

Manitoba Hardware, a small hardware distributor in Winnipeg, was forced to consider ways to reduce costs to remain profitable in a sluggish economy. The company took two actions related to employee benefits: (1) the company switched insurance carriers, and (2) employees were asked to pay for the formerly company-paid dental insurance benefit.

Disability and life insurance are big luxuries to the distressed firm. Those employees that wish to continue these benefits must pay the full cost.

Increase Waiting Period for Newly Hired Employees to Receive Coverage

Some companies provide benefits to the employee from the first day of hire, other firms have a "probationary" period, during which the new employee receives only a minimum of benefits. This waiting period is usually to allow both the employee and the employer to be certain there is a "good fit."

The additional value to the company of a waiting period is the cost savings from not having to provide full benefits for a few weeks or months. This is particularly relevant to retail and service companies, where employee-turnover rates exceeding 20% per annum are typical.

EFFECTS OF IMPLEMENTING A WAITING PERIOD FOR BENEFIT ELIGIBILITY FOR NEW HIRES (ASSUMES ANNUAL EMPLOYEE TURNOVER OF 20%)		
WAITING PERIOD	% ANNUAL SAVINGS PER NEW EMPLOYEE	% ANNUAL SAVINGS FOR COMPANY
1 month	8.3	1.7
2 months	16.7	3.3
3 months	25.2	5.0

Instituting a two-month waiting period for supplemental medical/dental insurance eligibility for new hires will reduce the cost of providing insurance for that employee, during the first year, by two-twelfths or almost 17%.

For a company with a 20% annual turnover of employees, a policy of waiting two months for insurance eligibility would result in annual savings of 3.3% of the cost of providing group medical insurance.

Give Employees Options

As a policy, it is politically unwise to eliminate types of coverage altogether; rather, the employer should provide for the option, where available, to allow the employee to continue uninterrupted coverage by directly paying the entire premium or by purchasing alternative or replacement coverage. This coverage can be purchased through payroll deduction using "pre-tax" dollars under current tax regulations.

The employer can also arrange with independent insurance agent(s) to meet with each employee, on an individual and confidential basis, to provide the employee with a variety of options to purchase replacement and alternative coverage.

One employer we knew that was forced to reduce significantly all employer-provided coverage provided an office, on-site, three mornings a week for an independent insurance agent to meet with interested employees during business hours to discuss replacement and alternative coverage.

The agent also arranged a group RRSP that provided low costs, numerous investment options, and an excellent program of low-cost term life insurance.

How to Tell Employees about Reduced Benefits

Although it is never easy to tell employees that they will be receiving less in their paycheque, the pain can be eased by using a positive approach when informing the employees. Explain the need for starting or increasing emloyee copayments in a positive way, as a method to save jobs and avoid layoffs, and you may ease the acceptance of, and reduce employee resentment to, the new policy.

It can also be useful to compare the company's benefits to other similar firms in the industry or the area, and demonstrate to employees that the company's benefits plan is still competitive.

Sick Leave and Vacation Pay

Vacation and sick leave affect both a company's balance sheet and its cash flow. In the long run, employees accumulating large quantities of vacation and sick leave add to the liabilities listed on the balance sheet and decrease the value of the company. However, in the near term, a company may want to deter employees from taking a vacation during a critical period when their absence would directly affect the firm's productivity and revenues.

Start by projecting the company's work flow for the next six months. If the company experiences a particularly slow period between Christmas and New Year or during the last two weeks of August, you may want to ask that all employees take their vacation during that period.

If the situation is critical enough, you may also want to ask even those employees who do not have earned vacation time accrued to take an unpaid vacation. If the policy is presented as being for the good of the company, most employees will accept it. How you present the policy to your employees will in large measure determine their response. See the section on alternatives to layoffs for a discussion of using forced leaves of absence and vacations to reduce labour costs. To reduce costs, Ontario did this in their new Social Contract, with many workers required to take 10 to 20 days of "vacation" without pay.

It can be less expensive for the company to insist as a matter of policy that employees use their vacation time each year and not "carry over" unused vacation leave for subsequent years.

An employee who uses accrued vacation time long after earning it costs the company more than the original value of the benefit, if the employee's salary or their value to the company has increased in the interim.

Remember that No Benefits Are Sacred Cows

Future vacation and future sick leave are not divinely ordained rights. They should not be treated as sacred cows. They are benefits given to employees for the company to remain competitive with its compensation package. Although it may appear to be difficult to reduce benefits for long-time employees, remember that these are the same employees who derived considerable benefit from the company's liberal policies during more prosperous times.

Start by instituting new rules for leave. With advance notice of a few months, advise all employees, in writing, that it will not be permissible to carry vacation and sick leave from year to year unless there are extenuating circumstances. The policy should be that all accrued leave must be used within twelve months of being earned.

Another common problem is that the highest salaried employees are the most likely to take longer vacations. In a troubled period there is nothing wrong with advising **all** employees, particularly management-level employees, that they cannot schedule more than five consecutive vacation days. Most will be motivated to stay for fear of losing their jobs while they are away.

Be wary of excessive sick leave. A simple but rigid policy of requiring a note from the employee's physician for more than two consecutive days of sick leave will reduce the abuse by dishonest employees without causing hardship to the honest ones. Companies may want to relax this rule during a period of flu or other common medical disorder. The results of a stringent sick leave policy will be cost savings and increased productivity.

All Other Visible Benefits: Pension Plans

Employer contributions to pension plans are not inviolate. The annual reports of many of Canada's largest corporations show unfunded liabilities to their pension funds. Borrowing from your employees' future to keep your firm alive is not the first choice, but if it becomes necessary, make the prudent choice. Large corporations including General Motors and Chrysler have enormous liabilities in this area.

Retirement Benefits

Who told you that the company must provide supplemental retirement benefits? According to a recent U.S. study,[4] 72% of very large firms (those with more than 5,000 employees) provide retiree health benefits, but only 37% of mid-size firms (those employing 200-999 workers) provide similar coverage. Furthermore, for the mid-size firms, the percentage providing coverage had declined from 44%. The study of over 1,000 firms reveals that even the percentage of large firms (1,000-4,999 workers) offering retiree health coverage is only 52%. While this only affects a few (7,500) Canadian companies, most pensioned workers expect this change as part of the new reality. Teachers, auto workers, and government employees all expect these changes in the 1990s.

The results of this study for troubled companies are that they don't need to offer retiree health benefits to remain competitive.

The study also discovered that 80% of all retiree benefits plans now require some copayment by the retiree. Contrast this statistic with that of a previous study, which showed that in 1985 most retirees who received health benefits did not pay any portion of the cost. Copayment for retirees has become widespread in a relatively short period of time.

For the troubled company, this means that if they haven't already implemented a copayment plan for retiree care benefits, now is the time to implement one, and instituting a copayment program or increasing the amount of copayment will not make the overall benefits package uncompetitive.

Subsidized Education

Most troubled companies should reduce, or at least temporarily suspend, all subsidies for education. Companies can suspend subsidies for a semester or two with a statement that the benefit will be reinstated after the company meets certain financial objectives.

One alternative is for companies to change the program to a "pooled" subsidy to fix and reduce costs. This means putting funds for educational subsidies into a pool and then allotting it to the employees who request the benefit on a prorated basis. In a semester when few employees request subsidies, most will receive the full benefit. However, in a semester when many employees request subsidies, the amount received will be only a partial subsidy.

Another alternative is to change from an advance payment to the employee to a reimbursement. This way, if the employee leaves the company, the risk of recovering monies advanced is reduced. Additionally, the company can shift current bills into the future, thereby freeing up additional cash flow for present and more important expenses.

Companies that need to eliminate or temporarily suspend the subsidy should make an effort to provide alternative sources of funds for their employees. Contact the local college's financial aid offices and seek the assistance of their financial-aid counsellors in providing alternatives to employees who will no longer be receiving subsidies. Management can also approach the company's bank for help in setting up a payroll deduction, or other educational loan plan, for employees.

Corporate Training

Correct and prudently timed training programs are valuable investments. The wrong training, or correct training at the wrong time, are wastes of a company's limited resources.

Carefully Evaluate Training Program

Carefully evaluate any educational and training programs that are in process or scheduled during the next twelve months. Remember that you are managing a company for survival, and those talents that are important to develop for a healthy company may not be the same talents that are required for the company to survive the next twelve months.

Seminars in gender-bias, business writing, and presentation skills are all very useful training programs, but none are likely to show enough of a return on the investment in the next six months to make them worthwhile.

Immediately cancel, delay, or reschedule (for the following year) those programs that are unnecessary for the company's survival and short-term future.

Increase Training Where Required   In examining the company you may discover an urgent need for additional training. Needs that are urgent can include requirements for training in customer service, purchasing, or security. Even under severe financial pressures, you may want to increase training in specific areas to reduce costs, protect assets, or increase revenues.

INVISIBLE BENEFITS

Although the term "invisible benefits" has been thrown about for some time, we doubt there is a formal definition. The benefits are invisible because, although they were voluntarily accepted by the employee, they are not usually detailed in the company's employee handbook as a listed employee benefit, are not generally perceived as a benefit, and the total cost of providing all of these benefits is rarely calculated.

Not all invisible benefits are legal. They often involve the conversion, knowingly or unknowingly, of company assets to personal property. In many cases, the shareholders would be upset to discover that employees are taking these "benefits," but the practice is either not expressly prohibited or is tolerated by management.

The list of what are invisible benefits is different for every industry, but the following list details some that are common to many businesses.

LIST OF COMMON INVISIBLE BENEFITS		
Personal Use of Company Assets	**Company Subsidized Services**	**Company Discounts for:**
Telephones	Health care facilities	Travel
Mails	Company nurse	Stores
Postage meters	Company physician	Museums
Courier services	Food services	
Facsimile machines	Coffee and snacks	
Photocopy machines	Vending machines	

Personal Use of Company Assets

Company Telephones

Every employee makes a few personal telephone calls from the office. Most companies permit the occasional personal use of their telephones, but for many firms employees abuse this benefit.

Some personal telephone calls may be permissible, but we agree with the findings of a study conducted by the American Banking Association in 1990. This study revealed that at many firms at least 25% of telecommunications costs are a result of nonbusiness-related calls. When was the last time your company audited its long-distance telephone bills? There are Canadian consultants whose entire practice is doing just this, and they make a fortune auditing bills and cutting costs.

Most employees who abuse the privilege do not perceive their use of the telephone as improper conduct. If you asked these employees if taking $25 a month from petty cash is stealing they would all agree with you, but ask them if it is permissible to call, from a company telephone, their mother-in-law in the next province, or their brother across the country, and they would minimize the cost and justify the expense. "Well, I was working late and I don't get paid overtime, so what's a few dollars of long-distance telephone calls...?" or, "My manager said I would have to work next weekend, so I thought it would be OK to call my fishing buddies and tell them that I wouldn't be at the lake."

At firms which do audit telephones, the system usually only monitors telephones at occupied desks. Conference rooms, storage rooms, vacant offices, and even elevators are often equipped with telephones which have unrestricted access. These can become potential targets for abuse by employees, janitorial staff, messengers, and visitors.

The problem in trying to regulate personal usage of company telephones is that managers are often the greatest offenders, since they know that no one is watching how much time they spend on the telephone. The solution has three parts: the policy, the carrot, and the stick.

The Policy: Start by telling each department manager that telecommunications costs need to be reduced. Explain that many employees are abusing the privilege of personal use of company telephones, and you want all managers to help in policing the company policy of only a few brief personal calls each day.

The Carrot: Tell the managers that the department with the most significant decrease in telecommunications costs for the next three months will receive a prize. Give the department a company-provided pizza lunch, or passes to a movie; make it something worth competing for without spending too much.

The Stick: See the section on "Reducing Telecommunications Costs" in Chapter 4 for a guide to auditing telephone invoices, and perform an audit for the previous month and for the next three to six months as required. Let the managers know you are watching and that the company will not tolerate abuse.

Postage Meter Abuses

Personal use of company postage machines can easily add 10% to 20% to your postal bill. This is most noticeable during the holiday season. We have observed employees staying late and putting hundreds of personal holiday greeting cards through the company postage meter.

The easiest way to eliminate postage abuse is to: (1) use the key that comes with the meter and lock the machine at night, and (2) place a sign beside the machine stating that **no** personal usage of the postage meter will be permitted. Let one employee take responsibility for the key and for locking the machine.

Courier Services

Employees and managers can easily avail themselves of the company's accounts for these expensive courier services and use them for personal mail and packages. Don't let it happen. Inform managers it will not be tolerated and, **most importantly, audit the invoices you receive from the couriers**. A few well-timed audits, for example, just after Christmas, will result in identifying the abusers and will send the proper message to the rest of the company that the practice will not be tolerated.

Emphasize Auditing All Invoices

The single best piece of advice that anyone can give you to detect abuse is to audit the company's invoices. Usually the abuses are not hidden and are glaringly obvious; it's just that no one is looking. Emphasize to all managers the need to review and approve invoices before the company will pay them.

How to Detect Abuse

If you are suspicious of the abuse of photocopy machines, fax machines, or postage meters, since these machines usually have mechanical or electronic counters, there is an easy method for detecting the abuse.

Since most of the abuse is done after hours, it is easy to detect. Leave the machine unlocked and have an "honest" employee keep a log book of meter readings at the end of every day and at the beginning of the next day. Although you will probably detect the abuse, you may not know the name of the abuser. Don't worry about it. As stated frequently in this book, the objective is to control costs, not locate abusive employees.

If abuse occurred, it was because management either didn't care, wasn't looking, or tolerated it. The objective of a company in trouble is to control costs and improve management, not to conduct a witch hunt.

Humour in the Troubled Company

"De Minimis Non Curat Lex" — *The Court Does Not Consider Trivial Matters.*

We are reminded of three examples where senior management wasted precious time looking for perpetrators of minor expense abuses, as if the individuals had committed a felony, instead of improving junior management and changing the procedures to prevent future abuse.

We will relate these stories for your amusement, as well as to remind you that management talent is too valuable an asset to waste.

Case #1

In *The Caine Mutiny*, by Herman Wouk, the captain, although admittedly paranoid, spent several months searching for the perpetrators of the theft of strawberries from the refrigerator in the officers' dining room. The captain was convinced there was a duplicate key to the refrigerator, but he never suggested the lock be changed or the mess sergeant assume responsibility for vigilance over the fruits.

Case #2

A women's garment manufacturer recently filed for bankruptcy protection, due to reported accounting irregularities. The problems were relatively serious for a public firm: what management (apparently) did was to report millions of dollars of profits for years, when they had a loss! And yet, according to reports, what did the directors concern themselves with at a meeting the week before the bankruptcy filing? Not the false financial statements, but the shortages that had been detected in the coin hopper of the telephone in the main lobby.

Case #3

Our own personal experience. A distribution and service company was facing an insolvency proceeding, with the potential of having a court-appointed receiver assume control of the business. The day before the court hearing, the CEO was absent from an important meeting with the company's legal counsel. A thorough search found the CEO in the company cafeteria, accusing the vending machine operator of short-changing the company on its cut of three soda machines.

If you detect abuse, then your first priority is to correct the problem that permitted the abuse to occur. Maybe next year you will have time to punish the abusers, but not today and probably not this year.

Subsidized Services and Company Discounts

Subsidized services are subject to two problems: abuse and lack of appreciation by employees. Abuse can be controlled by good security, and lack of appreciation can be corrected by the example of management and good communication.

To correct the problem of lack of appreciation, management must communicate with the employees the objective of the company in providing the subsidized or discounted service, the costs of providing it, and the benefits received.

The company can distribute memos, or post signs in the facility, detailing the objectives, the costs, and the benefits. If the employees don't appreciate the value they are receiving, it's usually because management has not set the proper example to follow.

The previous brief list of common invisible benefits includes health care facilities, company nurses, and company physicians as subsidized services. These are all good benefits to provide to your employees, if the company can afford them. For some companies, these health benefits can reduce the number of sick days and reduce health insurance costs. The problem with these benefits is that employees often fail to appreciate the value they are receiving. If the benefits are not resulting in costs savings and the employees are not appreciative, then the company should consider eliminating the benefit and saving the expense.

Benefits such as subsidized food services (cafeterias and kitchens), coffee and snacks, and vending machines are provided to employees and are sometimes appreciated and sometimes abused. Subsidized food services can be expensive to maintain and if not appreciated should be eliminated.

Company-provided discounts for travel (airline, automobile rental, and hotel, etc.), for shopping at stores, and for entrance to museums, can be of real value to its employees. Ask the vendors to let you know how much use was made of these discounts and what the value was that the employees received. Don't be shy! Let the employees know what a benevolent employer you are and the value they receive from the company's discounts.

Conclusions on Invisible Benefits

Be careful not to underestimate the magnitude of invisible benefits or the costs to the company. These benefits are very expensive and can make the difference between a profit and a loss.

INVISIBLE BENEFITS	
Are Typically	**But With Proper Management**
• Valuable to the employee	• Values can be communicated
• Unappreciated by employees	• Attitudes corrected by example
• Easily abused	• Auditing can control abuse
• Very costly to the company	• Costs can be limited and reduced

STRATEGY: EXPLORE ALTERNATIVES TO LAYOFFS

How Do Other Firms Avoid Layoffs?

A recent survey of 900 companies on workforce reductions reveals that 46% of companies had reduced their staffing levels during the last four years. Almost half the respondents used alternative strategies to reduce costs before resorting to firing employees.[5]

The following table illustrates the types of strategies utilized and the percentage of companies that used them.[6]

METHODS FOR PREVENTING LAYOFFS	%
Mandatory short work week/work day	15
Salary reductions or freezes	35
Demotion/downgrades/transfers to other jobs	44
Voluntary job sharing	15
Limited duration furloughs	14
Early retirement incentives	34
Voluntary separation plans	29

Additionally, 625 of the firms surveyed had implemented a freeze on new hiring. While a hiring freeze can initially control the need to terminate employees, it also constricts the flow of new employees and new ideas. A firm with a hiring freeze in effect for long periods may be inhibiting its future ability to grow and remain competitive.

Reducing the Work Week

Reducing the number of hours worked each week as an alternative to employee layoffs has been successfully used to reduce payroll costs for many years by Fortune 100 firms. Most small and mid-size firms, for an unknown reason, do not try reduced work weeks as an alternative employment strategy.

Reducing the work week is usually most effective where a company is experiencing a slowdown in business but wants to stay poised for future growth. Consider the savings: weekly payroll costs could be reduced by 20% for each day saved.

Companies can temporarily reduce the work week by moving to a three- or four-day week, or can reduce the total number of hours worked each week. When reducing the work week, there is no assurance that employees will stay with the company. However, with the alternative being employee terminations, most staff may be agreeable to stay and those that leave will do so voluntarily.

Large companies that have successfully implemented reduced work weeks to lower costs have included France's electronic giant Thomson, General Motors, and Boeing. Although in North America GM prefers to use layoffs and temporary plant closings to reduce costs, in Europe they have used reduced work weeks to achieve similar objectives. During January of 1993, a GM subsidiary in

Germany reduced the work week (calling it "short-time") to four-day weeks, for a period of three months, to reduce payroll costs.[7]

As mentioned earlier, the Ontario and British Columbia governments and Ontario Hydro are all following this model.

Boeing, the aircraft manufacturer, which was planning on reducing its workforce by more than 20,000 personnel, is experimenting with several forms of reduced work weeks as alternatives to layoffs.[8]

Workers at Thomson Electronics' main plant, outside Paris, recently agreed to a reduced work week as an alternative to company-forecasted massive layoffs. The employees agreed to accept a 45-minute-per-week reduction, totalling five fewer working days per year.[9] The annual savings to the company are estimated at 2% of total payroll costs.

In 1993 Data Switch Corp., faced with a downturn in sales of their computer products, took advantage of an innovative program in the State of Connecticut which allows employees to work reduced hours and be compensated by unemployment insurance for 70% of their pay for the remaining hours.

Where payroll represents the lion's share of overhead cost, a reduced work week may be a preferable alternative to layoffs.

Not all companies which consider reduced work weeks decide to implement them as alternatives to forced terminations. The problem of implementing a strategy of reduced work weeks is that it distributes the effect of cost savings over the entire workforce. Some companies have opted to insulate their best workers from these policies and prefer to lay off their less valuable employees.

In September of 1992, Software Publishing Corp., the publisher of Harvard Graphics, was faced with declining sales and increased competition and had to reduce costs. According to the *San Francisco Chronicle*, the company's senior management was very reluctant to implement layoffs and considered several alternatives, including waiting for natural attrition to reduce staffing and changing to a (reduced) four-day work week. After a careful analysis, the company decided to lay off 120 employees because, according to the CEO, management had reached the conclusion that the layoffs would "cause the least amount of pain with the maximum corporate gain."[10]

IBM Canada, Campbell Soup Canada, Petro-Canada, and Imperial Oil have all followed similar and correct rationales.

Salary Reductions or Freezes

Some firms have opted to reduce salaries in particular jobs or across the entire company as a method of reducing payroll while avoiding terminating employees. Hewlett Packard (HP), the computer giant, until the 1990s had a strong philosophy against layoffs. In the early 1970s, when HP's management recognized the need to reduce its workforce by 10% to meet its drop in sales, instead of laying off 10% of the staff, the entire company took a mandatory 10% reduction in pay. HP's management believed that by equally distributing the costs of the recession they would avoid the damage to a company's culture associated with layoffs.

HP's example has been followed by other technology companies seeking to reduce costs without losing productivity in a highly competitive marketplace. To avoid layoffs, Intel Corp. reduced salaries in 1983 by 10%; and in 1988, Hitachi reduced all management salaries by 5% to 10%.[11]

Not all management gurus agree with the technique of reducing salaries to avoid layoffs. They would argue that the trimming and pruning of employees (i.e., layoffs) to meet changing market conditions is necessary for the health of a company.

Supporters of these alternatives believe that by sharing the burden during hard times, companies can avoid the negative effects of layoffs, build employee loyalty and maintain the corporate "culture."

Reutilization of Employees

Where new employment opportunities exist for those about to be laid off, they should be offered swiftly and with respect. Even if the job is for less pay or lower status than the previous position, the company should allow the employee the chance to accept or reject the job. No man or woman will be humbled by accepting work as an alternative to unemployment to support their family.

Demotion or Transfer As an alternative to termination, the company can offer the employee an open position elsewhere in the company. Don't be afraid to offer a manager a staff position or a Toronto-based employee a position in Calgary. Employees are grateful that the company is trying to provide for them, even if the position is not the same status they were accustomed to. Confederation Life did just this and offered 300 positions in Saskatchewan to Toronto workers. Obviously, it was too little too late!

Tell Them to Move Quickly Any employees whom you want to use in other areas of the company or transfer to other offices should be informed immediately that a position is available and told they have only a few days to make a decision. If you allow too much time to decide, you might lose the opportunity to make the same offer to another qualified employee.

Loaning Employees An alternative to using the employee within the company is to place the employee with a customer or vendor on a temporary basis. This has been successfully done with technicians, customer service, and training personnel, who can be "loaned" or "rented" to customers or vendors for extended periods. In this way, the employee does not lose their seniority or benefits status and the company does not necessarily lose the loyalty of the worker. There is a risk that the employee will decide not to return, but it is still a better alternative than forced unemployment.

General Motors, not usually the company to employ innovative personnel management practices, recently began pushing a new plan for finding jobs for workers laid off by GM with their suppliers. The program being directed by the purchasing department is called the "strategic insourcing initiative." Under the program, suppliers can use GM facilities as an incentive to hire laid-off GM employees and use laid-off GM employees for temporary help. By 1994, GM had six "insourcing" agreements with suppliers.[12]

Early Retirement and Voluntary Separation

Many companies who are reluctant to lay off staff, for fear of upsetting the corporate culture, have offered early retirement to their employees. Early retirement programs, called "voluntary separation" packages, can be combined with outplacement assistance to find the "retirees" new employment.

Many troubled companies can barely afford their payroll and could not afford the costs of severance for a voluntary separation program, but for those with deep enough pockets it is an alternative to mandatory layoffs.

To avoid its first-ever layoff, during 1989 and 1990 Digital Equipment Corporation offered a voluntary separation (retirement) benefits package for any employee who was at least 50 years old with at least five years of service. Benefits included severance pay ranging from 13 weeks (for 2 years of service) to 77 weeks (for 20 years), outplacement assistance, and health insurance. More than 5,500 employees took the voluntary separation package. Industry sources say that the contribution to cost savings of these voluntary departures allowed Digital to avoid its first layoffs for an additional two years.[13] Ontario Hydro followed a similar scheme in its voluntary retirement plan for 5,000 workers.

Some companies that introduced early-retirement packages were surprised by the volume of response. Dupont, which originally expected 6,500 employees to accept the plan, was surprised when more than twice that number volunteered. Unfortunately for Dupont, they lost some key employees that they had wanted to keep.

The problem of valuable employees accepting early retirement can be avoided by management attention to preparing employees for the coming changes. Management can use subtle persuasion to induce employees to stay or to leave and to "fine tune" the technique to achieve their objectives.

Voluntary Job Sharing

Job sharing is where two employees divide the work, the pay, and the benefits of one job between themselves. Although not commonly used, job sharing has recently become more popular and was an alternative used by 15% of the firms in a recent survey of companies that laid off employees. Job sharing can be an attractive alternative employment strategy. Teachers, auto workers, and engineers have followed similar programs, where UIC is used to top up earnings or provincial government programs pay a partial subsidy to keep both workers on the job part-time.

One prime example of a successful job sharing program is Polaroid Corporation. Polaroid has designed jobs so that employees alternate on either half-day or every-other-day schedules. Although most of Polaroid's job sharers are hourly factory workers, the approach could work for more senior employees. Other companies promoting job sharing as an alternative to layoffs are Bell South, Boeing, and General Motors.

Limited Duration Furloughs

Temporary layoffs, or furloughs, can include forced vacations or unpaid leaves of absence. Companies which have recently used unpaid leaves of absence to reduce costs have included Polaroid, Pacific Northwest Bell, Amdahl, and Hewlett Packard.

Where the variable costs of operating are high and would immediately be reduced by a temporary closing of facilities, the option of closing the company and temporarily furloughing all employees should be explored. This technique has primarily been used by large industrial firms, but small- and medium-sized firms may also find value in closing offices and facilities for several weeks during holidays or slow seasons.

Companies which use temporary closings to furlough staff during periods of business slowdowns include the major airlines, auto manufacturers, and aircraft manufacturers.

TERMINATING EMPLOYEES

Where redundancy is present, or employees can be readily replaced, companies may choose to layoff portions of their staff. **WARNING: The emotional cost of firing employees can be significant.** But it is better to reduce a company's costs by laying off 20% and remain healthy than to be forced out of business and put 100% of the employees out of work.

One business author has said, "Firing is one of the crucibles that turn entrepreneurs into managers, because it brings you face-to-face with failure. Nothing will make firing any easier. It shouldn't get easier. What it should become is less frequent."[14]

Before making any decisions to lay off employees, first examine methods for reducing costs and increasing revenues. Changes in costs and revenues may result in your making different choices on which employees to lay off.

It's a Dirty Job, But Someone Has To Do It

As a manager, do not avoid your responsibilities when it becomes necessary to discharge employees. Don't confuse your sympathy for the employee with the necessity of sound business judgement. A profitable business that only requires 50 employees, is "troubled" and may be unprofitable supporting a payroll of 60 persons.

The first time through a firing is a painful exercise. No one can possibly look forward to terminating long-term, loyal staff who have few employment alternatives. Personal experience shows that we had migraines before and sleeplessness afterwards. No one grows to like it or find it a comfortable experience.

When there is a troubled situation, many workers will be aware of it. Most will be sensitive to the problems management is experiencing, and many will be relieved to know they are being let go with a reasonable severance rather than getting terminated without pay in a bankruptcy liquidation.

Once the decision has been made to terminate an employee, there are some basic rules that we can offer the manager charged with the responsibility of informing a subordinate. Using these rules will give you a script to follow and help to make the process efficient and expeditious. The standard rules of good management apply when terminating employees. A good manager should be effective and compassionate, yet remain firm when executing sound business decisions.

Scheduling the Termination Meeting

Don't wait until weeks after the decision has been made to inform the employee. Bad news travels fast, and even waiting a few days may be enough time for the employee to have heard "through the grapevine" instead of hearing it from you. The meeting should be held as soon as possible after the decision.

Try to choose a day for the meeting towards the latter part of the week. This way if there is any internal "fallout," it won't interfere with job performance during the week and, after a weekend has elapsed, the effect will be further reduced.

Choose a time after lunch; people are more relaxed after eating, and if they react with strong emotions to the news, they can leave the office early without losing face or disturbing the work flow.

What You Need To Be Prepared

When meeting with an employee to inform them of their imminent termination, you should be prepared with four documents which will provide you with a script to follow during the meeting. These documents should be contained in a closed manilla folder to be presented to the employee at the conclusion of your meeting. Retain a duplicate copy of each document for your own records.

The documents are: (1) a formal signed letter of termination, (2) a statement of accrued and termination benefits, (3) a copy of the company policy regarding termination, and (4) a letter of recommendation.

Termination Letter

A termination letter is a very succinct one-paragraph document. The letter is addressed to the employee informing them that they have been terminated with a clear statement of the reasons and the effective date.

In the case of a troubled business, the letter should state that the employee was terminated because the company's business has declined (or the division is being closed, or the work is being transferred to another location, etc.) and, therefore, the individual's services are no longer required.

The letter should briefly thank the employee for their years of service and inform them that they can discuss their termination benefits with the personnel department (or whomever is the designated benefits contact person).

The Statement of Benefits

The employee's statement of accrued and termination benefits should detail all salary, commissions, vacation pay, paid sick leave, and expense reimbursement owed to the employee as of the effective date of their termination. Remember the statutory notice periods. The statement should also include any termination benefits and insurance conversion rights, retirement and pension plan rights, and severance pay.

With the severance package, offer long-term workers financial planning counselling to reduce their taxes and to maximize their RRSP contributions. Many investment firms offer free in-house seminars for workers receiving substantial severances or those with retirement planning needs. Seminar providers include Fortune Financial, Financial Concepts Group, A.I.C., and Planvest.

Be certain that the statement includes debits for monies the employee owes to the company including cash advances, loans, or vacation or sick leave taken before being earned.

If the employee has equipment in their personal possession such as a computer, fax machine, cellular telephone, or pager, then this equipment should be detailed on the statement, along with a note that the final cheque will not be given to the employee until the equipment listed has been returned to the company. Equipment is an asset of the company and while in the possession of the employee is a liability that the employee owes to the company.

If the termination is effective on the same day or the next day and the employee has no outstanding liabilities to the company, then it is good form to present the employee, at the meeting, with a cheque for the full amount owed to them (except for severance benefits).

The Company Policy Regarding Termination

If the company has an employee handbook or a policy manual detailing the policy towards terminated employees, include a copy of these policies along with the statement of benefits. This will avoid any confusion that may arise. Employees often confuse what they have "heard" about termination benefits with the official policy of the company.

The Letter of Recommendation

All employees, except those terminated for gross incompetence or criminal activity or those that have worked for the company for less than three months, deserve a letter of recommendation to use when looking for future employment. Writing a letter of recommendation will lessen the traumatic effects of the firing to the employee and will serve as good public relations to the surviving employees, showing that they will be well treated when they leave. You also want to avoid the so called "grudge factor," the resentment that employees feel when one of their colleagues is fired or treated unfairly. These grudges can affect morale and reduce employee productivity.

A letter of recommendation also increases the efficiency of the termination process because it avoids the necessity of the employee coming back to ask for a letter, next week, next month, or next year.

Keep the letter to less than one page in length. Detail the length of the employee's tenure with the company, the initial and final positions they held, and the types of work they were responsible for. Do not put any negative comments into the letter. Your writing should accent the employee's strengths, their hard work, attitude, and commitment. The letter should be addressed to whom it may concern and be signed by the most senior person in the firm who had knowledge of the employee's performance.

The letter should not discuss the reasons for the employee's discharge. Your statement that you would recommend the individual for another position, and not the reasons leading up to their departure, is the primary purpose of this letter.

STEP-BY-STEP GUIDE TO TERMINATING EMPLOYEES

1. Schedule the meeting as soon as possible after the decision has been made. Try for a time towards the end of the week, preferably after lunch. Do not give the employee advance warning of what is to be discussed at the meeting.

   Some managers prefer to conduct the meeting in surroundings that are familiar to the employee. You may want to meet with the employee in their office or in a private conference room near their desk or work area.

2. In advance, inform the person responsible for benefits and have them prepare the statement of accrued and termination benefits for presentation to the employee.

   Have the statement double-checked, and if you have reason to believe that the employee will question or disagree with the statement, then attach a copy of the supporting documentation.

3. Be prepared for your meeting.
   Have your documents ready:
   • a formal signed letter of termination;
   • a statement of accrued and termination benefits;
   • a copy of the company policy regarding termination;
   • a letter of recommendation.

4. Be serious about your role. Be yourself, but be formal. Make certain that you will not be disturbed by interruptions during the meeting. Open the meeting by informing the employee that because of the economic pressures facing the company, it is no longer possible to retain their valued services and that they are being terminated as of the effective date.

5. Thank them for their years of service and their hard work. Open the folder on your desk containing the four documents and tell them that the folder is for them and that it contains a letter of termination and a letter of recommendation to assist them in obtaining a new position.

   Don't give them the folder until the meeting is at the conclusion; they'll have plenty of time to read the enclosures during the next few days.

6. Inform the employee they are entitled to certain accrued and termination benefits, which are detailed in the benefits statement also enclosed in the folder, and that they can discuss the details with the designated benefits person in the company. Also enclosed in the folder, for their reference, is a copy of the company's policy on terminated employees.

7. Advise the employee that you expect they will perform the responsibilities of their position in a professional manner during their remaining tenure.

    Wish them well and then stand up, shake their hand and either show them to the door or if you are in their office, leave the room. Don't linger in the area and chat with other employees; you can always return in an hour. Let the discharged employee inform his colleagues in person.

8. Most importantly, keep the meeting brief. There is nothing you can tell them that isn't contained in the folder you are presenting to them and little you can do for them unless you have an out-placement program.

    The longer the employee sits in your office, the more likely they are to become emotional. You are not being insensitive by leaving. Being fired is, indeed, an emotional experience, but not one that you as a manager should be sharing with your employee.

Outplacement

Laying off employees is never easy, though if the employee is qualified you can make the process easier for the employee and earn considerable goodwill in your company by providing formalized or personal outplacement services.

Outplacement is providing assistance to an employee to obtain a new position. You can do this by making telephone calls through your personal or business contacts. There are also employment search firms and agencies which specialize in out-placement that can assist companies in trying to place employees whose services are no longer required.

To maintain company morale among those not laid off and to present a positive public image, many firms provide some form of outplacement counselling or job-assistance benefits for their laid-off employees.

The last few years has seen the emergence of specialized outplacement consulting firms to provide these services.[15] Some cities and provinces will also provide outplacement assistance to companies that will be laying off large numbers of employees.

Proactive companies have even taken out advertisements in newspapers and trade journals soliciting potential employers to call special hotlines, voluntarily staffed by the laid-off employees, to hire laid-off employees.

Hewlett-Packard, known for it's innovative personnel policies, recently germinated two small businesses to provide jobs for employees from departments that were going to be reduced or terminated. The departments provided internal training and technical writing services to the company. The departing employees accepted reduced salaries and benefits, but they did not have to face the prospect of unemployment.[16]

Research among fired managers shows that many would rather have more cash in their severance as an option/alternative to the services of an outplacement firm. The cost of these firms can be up to $20,000 per manager versus $5,000 cash to workers as an alternative.

We recently completed a survey of 300 Canadian managers who received outplacement. Most (nearly 70%) said they preferred the cash value of the outplacement. This is a huge industry that has grown enormously since 1988. Ask workers what they would prefer. Local community colleges can offer career and seminar courses for a lower cost to you.

NOTES

[1]*The Financial Post*, April 14, 1993, p.6, "400 firms to cut staff to aid profit," Joanne Chianello. Quoting a study of 505 firms in layoffs and profitability by Right Associates, an outplacement consulting firm, and *The San Francisco Chronicle*, October 26, 1992, quoting an American Management Association survey of 836 U.S.-based companies on workforce reductions that occurred between July 1991 and July 1992.

Managers may also want to read *Downsizing* by Robert Tomasko. (New York: American Management Association, 1987, updated edition 1989). This is an excellent book on streamlining companies for future growth and competitiveness. The author explores the risks of layoffs to achieve cost reductions and alternative strategies that companies should consider.

[2]*The San Francisco Chronicle*, October 26, 1992, p.B-1, "Downsizing Corporate America: Cost-cutting trend sparks a workplace revolution," Jeff Pelline and Kenneth Howe.

[3]*Industry Week*, August 3, 1992, Penton/IPC, p.14, Downsizing section, "Managing survivors," Brian S. Moskal.

[4]"Retiree Health Benefits: An Era of Uncertainty," 1993, KPMG Peat Marwick, Newark, N.J.

[5]The contemporary human resources euphemism for "firing" employees is "involuntary termination." Although the term is commonly used, it reminds us of murder. It sounds like Ian Fleming's James Bond 007 dialogue about an assassination, in which the act is called "termination with extreme prejudice."

[6]*The Financial Post*, April 14, 1993, p.6, "400 firms to cut staff to aid profit," Joanne Chianello.

[7]Reuters Wire, January 14, 1993, "GM unit extends short time work hours."

[8]*The Seattle Times*, April 27, 1993, p.D-8, "Boeing options may help reduce layoffs," Polly Lane.

[9]United Press International, March 17, 1993, "Employees at Thomson choose fewer hours over unemployment," Molly Schuetz.

[10]*The San Francisco Chronicle*, October 26, 1992.

[11]*Compensation and Benefits Review,* American Management Association (AMA), July 1991, Vol.23/No.4, p.33, "Downsizing: AMA survey results," Eric Rolfe Greenberg, and p.19 "Downsizing: layoffs and alternatives to layoffs," Robert M. Tomasko.

[12]*Automotive News*, February 1, 1993, p.4, "GM asks suppliers to use its laid-off workers."
The designer of this innovative strategy was none other than Jose Lopez de Arriotua, then GM's vice president in charge of worldwide purchasing, who would become the centre of the controversy surrounding his decision to leave GM for Volkswagen.

[13]In 1991, when DEC was finally forced to lay off employees, all of the 6,900 employees laid off received the same severance package that they had been offered previously for voluntary separation.

[14]*Inc.*, May 1992, p.67, "How to fire," Karen E. Carney.

[15]Many companies now provide outplacement assistance as part of their severance package for laid-off employees. Large companies that recently provided these services to their employees include Eckerd Drugs, Lockheed, Macy's, General Electric, Boeing, General Motors, and Safeway. However, outplacement is no longer limited just to large firms; small and mid-sized firms and even nonprofits are turning more toward the use of specialized outplacement firms as a more humane way of taking care of discharged employees. The outplacement consulting business, which was in its infancy during the 1980s, was estimated to have had a gross revenue in 1992 of $600 million. See *Crains New York Business*, September 14, 1992, p.12, "Fast starter sees outplacement slowing," Alan Breznick.

[16]*Boston Globe*, April 4, 1993, p.80, "In lieu of layoffs."

CHAPTER 10

SELLING YOUR BUSINESS*

WHEN CREDITORS are knocking at your door and there is no money to pay the bills, do not despair. Although your company is in distress, you may still be able to sell it. You may think the business is worthless; however, your misfortune may be a timely opportunity for someone else.

The blood, sweat, and tears invested in starting a business are often worth more to a potential buyer than an owner of a troubled business realizes. They have a valuable property to offer: a fully equipped and operational business with an established base of customers. It is a good story to tell: the company worked hard to get to where it is, but along the way, it ran into some problems. The company still has good prospects, the business is still viable, and it is searching for the right partner. With good marketing and a positive attitude, a troubled business can often be sold for more than its "book" value.

No business, least of all a troubled one, can be sold overnight. It requires a series of steps, a process: locating and recruiting potential purchasers, building trust, performing due diligence, validating the business, confirming the financing, negotiating the price, agreeing to terms, and then consummating the sale. Whether you are selling the entire business or parts of it, or are seeking financial investment into your business, the process is

---

* Parts of this chapter were adapted from Matthew L. Shuchman, "Selling Points", *Entrepreneur*, July 1994.

Exhibit 10-1

STEPS IN SELLING A BUSINESS		
BUYER'S ROLE	PROCESS STEP	SELLER'S ROLE
	MARKETING	
What's for Sale?	Confidentiality Agreement	Locate & Recruit
Can We Afford It?	Sales Memorandum	Prospects
		Qualify Prospects
	SALES	
Is the Business Viable?	Building Confidence	Tell Your Story!
Do We Want It?	Letter of Understanding	What Do They Really
Worth Looking Further?		Want?
		What Do We Want?
	DUE DILIGENCE	
Verify Financials	Escrow Agreement	Use Supporting
& Business	Deposit Escrow	Documents
Obtain Approvals	Provide Documentation	Want This Deal?
Confirm Financing	Negotiate Final Terms	Is It a Good Fit?
	& Conditions	
	CLOSING	
Purchase!	Contract	Sale!

very similar. The following diagram outlines the basic steps in selling a troubled business.

MARKETING YOUR BUSINESS

The sales memorandum is the most important document in selling any business. This three- to four-page summary answers the questions: What's for sale? and, why would someone be interested in buying? One consultant who has been involved with many sales of troubled companies says, "To maximize its value, the owners of a troubled company should be selling not just the assets, but their vision of the future and their plan for how the business can achieve it." The sales memorandum together with certain lists (customers, inventories, etc.), legal documents (leases, contracts, loan agreements, etc.), and financial reports should tell a convincing story about the company.

OUTLINE FOR A SALES MEMORANDUM

1. What is for sale?
   - Describe the business and list of assets.
   - State sales for last three years and current forecast.
   - List customers, staff, plant and equipment.
2. Why is it for sale?
3. State sales price and terms.
4. Describe potential purchasers.
5. Give brief history (founding, achievements, mission statement).
6. Whom should they contact?

What Is for Sale?   Are you selling the entire business? Inventory? Just the customer list? **Describe the business** offered for sale and the **list of assets** included. Briefly discuss the **sales for the last three years** and your **current forecast**. How large is the company? Provide a thumbnail sketch of the company including the number and types of: **customers** and **staff**; and a list of **plant and equipment**.

Why Is It for Sale?   Tell a story that a prudent businessperson would believe. Be honest and sound credible. Good reasons are the retirement or illness of the principals, the lease has expired, the company grew too fast, or the need for additional working capital (i.e., creditors are becoming hostile or the burden of past due taxes is crushing).

Sales Price and Terms   Don't be too detailed but let the reader know if they qualify as potential purchasers. Give a price range, list fixed terms and assets, and the future availability of the principals. Is there a bank loan or mortgage which the new owner could assume? What is the minimum cash payment required? If you have an overdue tax payment of $200,000, then don't be shy. Tell potential buyers that at least $200,000 of the sale price is required to be in cash. Let the buyer know the framework you want to work in. Defining price and terms clearly can avoid those "You never told me it had to be an all cash offer!" problems.

Who Are the Potential Purchasers   Who would be interested in purchasing the company? Let the reader know they are included: a firm in the same business, a complementary business, or an entity with specific investment objectives.

Brief Corporate History of the Company   In one or two paragraphs bring the reader up to date, explaining **how the company was founded** and including any **significant achievements since its founding.** Include the company's **mission statement** and how this relates to the company's **current focus.**

The following is a good example of a brief corporate history of the fictional EZ Oil Change company:

> EZ Oil Change, Inc. was founded and financed in 1986 by two former automobile mechanics to provide rapid and inexpensive oil changes for passenger cars on the north shore of Montreal. In 1987 it opened its first location and has opened one new location every two years since its founding. Currently the company is enhancing each location to add tire sales and service.

Who Should Be Contacted?   Will you speak to potential purchasers, or would you prefer that your lawyer or business broker screen and qualify them first? (A well-designed screening process can save considerable time.)

LOCATING POTENTIAL PURCHASERS

Potential purchasers are easy to approach if you have a good story to tell. Start by approaching the contacts you have in every-day business.

POTENTIAL PURCHASERS
• Major suppliers
• Major competitors of your suppliers
• Competitors
• Business in related areas
• Executives from your industry
• Major creditors
• Major customers

Major Suppliers

A major vendor or supplier of your company is an ideal candidate to invest in your firm. As long as you stay in business, and purchase products from them, they will prosper. Many suppliers are reluctant to invest in any one of their customers for fear of alienating another customer, but this rule does not apply if your firm has an exclusive (contractual or de facto) arrangement with the supplier for a particular market. Even if they cannot directly make an investment they may be an excellent source of leads to other potential investors.

Major Competitors of Your Suppliers

If your major supplier is not interested or is not approachable as a potential investor, then consider your supplier's competition. This is not a disloyal act — it is a question of survival!

If you currently sell one brand of personal computers and neither the manufacturer nor the distributor can assist you financially, then discreetly approach the manufacturer and the distributor of competing product lines. The competitor of your supplier may have been scheming for years on how to "steal" you away from your current supplier and grow you as a customer. He has a very large incentive to assist you: His reward will be your future business.

Competitors

Surprisingly to many troubled companies, the most unlikely parties, your present competitors, can become your natural allies in the business of survival. By purchasing your company, your competitor can eliminate your threat as competition while securing your relationship as a "friendly" colleague.

The first objective in this process is to properly identify your competitors. Who are your competitors? Make a list of your current competitors.

"WE DON'T HAVE ANY COMPETITORS..."

More than one business owner has told me that they didn't have any competitors. They admitted there were other firms in similar businesses, but insisted that these firms couldn't provide the same quality of service. Saying that you don't have any competitors is a falsehood and a myth to hide behind.

With very few exceptions, all businesses have competitors. You may not perceive that they provide the products and services in the same way as your firm, but they are still your competition. Don't let your ego or your image of the company interfere with your judgement of who your competitor is.

Ask yourself the question: If you were to shut your doors tomorrow, who would your customers turn to as a replacement for your company?

Who Are They?

Assemble a brief dossier on each of your competitors. This dossier should include: company name, addresses, names of principals and senior managers, telephone and facsimile numbers, number of employees, breakdown of staff (management, professional, support, etc.), estimated annual sales, type of ownership (public, private), principals, major customers, authorized dealerships or specialties, and their current business profile.

EXHIBIT 10-2

WHY IT IS IMPORTANT TO KNOW YOUR COMPETITION

The company's competitors are valuable for many reasons: (1) as joint venture partners, (2) as customers for excess inventory, (3) destinations for the outplacement of employees, and (4) as potential buyers for the business.

1. Competitors can be helpful in situations where your firm is no longer able to operate independently. These "joint ventures" may be a business opportunity that is outside of your regional service area or a project that is too big for your firm.

2. Should you have excess inventory of spare parts, new merchandise, or used equipment, your prime customers for the excess inventory could be your competition.

3. If you need to lay off employees because you are terminating a division, there is no harm in contacting your competitors, who could utilize your loyal employees.

4. If you decide to sell all or part of your business, your competitor is an ideal candidate to be a potential purchaser.

If you don't know your competitors personally, don't wait any longer; seek them out. Don't let your ego get in your way. You don't need an intermediary. They probably know who you are, so they are likely to return your telephone call. Meet them now. Have a drink with them. Don't wait until the last moment, you may lose valuable opportunities in the interim.

W A R N I N G

Be very guarded in your approaches to your competitors, they are in a strategic position to exploit the information you reveal to them about your precarious financial condition.

The discussion at the first meeting with a competitor should concentrate on the strengths of a union between the firms, the ability to devote the combined efforts at obtaining new business, the power of the combined resources, and the synergy of all the excellent talent available to the potential union. Don't go too heavily into a discussion of your company's immediate financial needs. Describe your company's needs for additional working capital to grow to the next stage to achieve dreams that both you and your competitor share in common.

If there is strong interest from a competitor in a potential union, then seek legal counsel and protection immediately.

PROTECT YOUR COMPANY

First and foremost, your competitor must execute a confidentiality, nondisclosure, and noncircumvention agreement. The document should state clearly that the only reason for exchanging information with your competitor is the furtherance of ventures which profit both parties.

Secondly, if you are selling any inventory, fixed assets, or spare parts to your competitor make certain the payment terms are cash, bank, or certified cheque. Particularly if you have creditors, the sale of assets (though not intended to defraud your creditors) could raise some eyebrows with a nasty creditor, or an unscrupulous competitor could cause the payments to be frozen or redirected away from your company at a critical time.

Many is the company that considered purchasing a troubled colleague in another region and failed to consummate the transaction. Within a year, they had established operations in direct competition, having learned the recipe for success during the prior due-diligence period. Though the troubled company can respond with litigation, they have already suffered the damage.

The lesson to be learned is that legal protection is a requirement, but there is no substitute for carefully evaluating a potential purchaser and their motivation. If the potential purchaser believes they can achieve the same strategic or financial objectives without acquiring your company, they probably will.

Businesses in Related Areas   Businesses in related areas are potential competitors, but for reasons of geography or market specialization they do not directly compete with you in your marketplace. They may be a dealer of the same or similar product lines located in another major city; a business which sells the same services as your firm but only to residential customers, where your company sells exclusively to commercial customers; or, a business which sells the same products exclusively by mail-order that you sell directly.

Executives from Your Industry   These executives can be a valuable and knowledgeable talent pool and may provide the added confidence necessary to attract investors.

Major Creditors   Unless you are a very large company or your creditor is also a supplier, major creditors are unlikely to be interested in being investors. You should still approach them as they may have leads to pursue potential investors.

W A R N I N G

When your business is close to insolvency, do not reveal this information to a major creditor, unless the revelation is part of a renegotiation strategy. Creditors with knowledge of your pending insolvency will act to protect their own interests. Failure to disclose potential insolvency is only relevant when dealing with a new creditor or leader.

The acts of a major creditor with knowledge of your insolvency can include a refusal to provide additional financing, freezing of bank accounts, and a lack of flexibility with payment terms. In the most severe cases, they can initiate insolvency proceedings which can lead to a court-appointed receivership or an involuntary bankruptcy filing.

Major Customers Don't ignore your major customers as potential investors. Your customers know your story, they know the service that you can deliver and your commitment to the business. The question your customer will ask is "Why?" and, assuming they can understand your story, they will need to decide if the investment is prudent for them. Don't be too afraid to reveal the way you do business to your customers; they are aware that you need to make a profit to survive.

> ### W A R N I N G
> Do not reveal so much information to your customer that they will fear your continued survival, and don't approach them unless you have a strong and secure relationship with them. A dissatisfied customer with knowledge of your business can hurt you even more than a competitor.

Using Business Brokers

If you are unable to locate qualified candidates, or need to shield your identity, then don't hesitate to involve a business broker or independent third party early in the process. Experiences with business brokers vary, but it is important to find one who understands your business. Stephen Hopkins, president of the turnaround consulting firm Nightingale Associates says, "Typical business brokers don't know your business and you may do better with an informed third party, like your accountant or lawyer, who understands your company."

Investment Banks

You may also want to consider the traditional investors in privately owned companies: venture capital funds and investment groups. These financial players will only be interested if your company is large enough in your industry to be significant; owns valuable rights, franchises, or patents; or is developing a new technology that could revolutionize your industry.

Investment firms can also be a valuable source for leads to potential buyers and may broker the sale (for a commission). These firms are experienced at buying and selling businesses and can also provide a critical review of your sales memorandum.

Prepare Documents to Support Your Story

In addition to the sales memorandum, many confidential documents will be requested during the sales process or the subsequent due-diligence period. These documents should answer most of the financial and legal questions about the business. Give the buyer confidence there are no hidden surprises. Gather and place the supporting documents into notebooks with tables of contents and index tabs for a professional appearance.

CONTENTS OF NOTEBOOKS FOR POTENTIAL PURCHASERS

1. Confidentiality Agreement
2. Sales Memorandum
3. Financials
   - Summary of Financials (textual)
     –what happened
     –what is and what is not included, and why
     –general assumptions
   - Income/Expense Statements and Projections
   - Cash Flow Statements and Projections
   - Balance Sheet and Assumptions
4. Lists of fixed assets, inventory, suppliers, customers
5. Legal documents: leases, contracts, mortgages, loans, and insurance policies
6. Federal, provincial, and local tax returns
7. Summary of outstanding litigation
8. Public relations (press releases, brochures, etc.)
9. Biographies of senior management.

Which documents to include depends on the type of sale, the buyer's sophistication, and the ability to assemble the materials. These documents are marketing tools; they should tell the truth, but sell the company's vision. In the absence of any of the critical documents, be prepared with explanations which would make sense to a prudent and reasonable businessperson.

Exhibit 10-3 details the historical period for each category of document and the period that is desirable to meet the requirements of the more detail-oriented purchaser or investor.

EXHIBIT 10-3

REQUIRED VS. DESIRABLE DOCUMENTS FOR INVESTORS		
DESCRIPTION	REQUIRED	DESIRABLE
Sales Memorandum	current	N/A
Balance Sheet period	annually	quarterly
Balance Sheet history	current	last 3 yrs
List of fixed assets	current	N/A
List of inventory	current	last year-end
Income Statement period	yr-to-date	monthly
Income Statement history	last yr	last 3 yrs
Income projections	next 6 mos	next 12 mos
Annual cash flows	yr-to-date	last 3 yrs
Monthly cash flows	last 6 mos	last 12 mos
Monthly cash flow forecast	next 3 mos	next 12 mos
List of suppliers and vendors	current	last 2 yrs
List of customers	current	last 3 yrs
Leases and contracts	current	N/A
List of competitors	current	last 2 yrs
Mortgages and loans	current	possibly
Federal tax returns	possibly	possibly
Provincial tax returns	possibly	possibly
Insurance policies	current	N/A
Corporate records	possibly	N/A
Summary of outstanding litigation	current	N/A

DUE DILIGENCE

"Due diligence" is the period and process during which the buyer and seller, having agreed to the sale, review the confidential legal, financial, and business documentation supporting the claims and statements made by the seller in the sales memorandum and in oral presentations. Adjustments to the terms and conditions of the final agreement are predicated on new discoveries made during the process. Turnaround honcho Stephen Hopkins warns sellers, "Don't let due diligence proceed until you have agreed to the terms of a sale."

Due diligence should **always** be preceded by the execution of a letter of understanding regarding the interest of both parties in consummating a transaction, with the approximate sale price, terms, and most importantly, the **timing** necessary. Don't wait until after due diligence to agree on a price. Says Hopkins, "All due diligence should do is to confirm the buyer's understanding of the representations you have made about the business, its assets, and its earnings power."

Trust and "Kill Fees"

In conjunction with the letter of understanding, the seller should demand the buyer deposit funds in a trust account. The trust's purpose is two-fold: (1) as a sign of good faith by the purchaser; and (2) as insurance ("kill fee"). If the buyer fails to act in "good faith," is unable to obtain financing, or is responsible for unauthorized delays, their actions could trigger the release of trust to the seller as a kill fee. A written agreement should detail the terms under which the trust deposit is made, the money is to be released, and to whom the funds are to be released.

There is no set rules specifying the terms and conditions of a trust agreement. The rules are dictated by the level of comfort that you feel with regard to the potential purchaser. The more uncomfortable you are with the potential purchaser, the more stringent should be the conditions of the agreement. If the potential purchaser truly intends to make an investment, then the conditions under which the deposit would be forfeited will not matter as much to them.

An additional deposit is recommended if the buyer's requests place the seller at risk. For example, in buying a service business, the final step would be to meet with selected customers. Although the request is not unreasonable, should the buyer decide not to proceed, the business could suffer irreparable harm. As compensation for this risk, sellers should not hesitate to require an additional deposit.

What Will the Buyer Ask?

After reviewing documents, buyers will ask many questions. Listen carefully, but remember: there is no requirement for you to answer all the inquiries. Tell your story honestly and be clear that there is nothing to hide. **More deals are killed by a lack of candour than by a lack of lustre.** If the story sounds too good, they will ask why you need a buyer, and if it's too distressing they will be concerned there isn't enough time to save the business.

Don't approach due diligence with a fear of how to explain past failures. You can't change history. Every business makes mistakes. Rarely is it one large error in judgement or a wrong decision that leads to the failure of a business. More commonly the causes of failure were several smaller mistakes whose consequences were ignored or overlooked. Be cognizant of the company's woes, but respond to questions about past problems with a marketing pitch highlighting recent successes, e.g., "Yes, transportation costs were high, but we recently subcontracted trucking and expect to realize significant savings next year."

Have someone whose criticism you value review your documents and list questions a sceptical businessperson would ask. Preparing succinct and believable answers to these questions will increase the chances of a smooth due-diligence process.

What You Should and Shouldn't Say

Buyers are concerned that once a business is sold, its employees will quit and its customers will evaporate. Your job is to convince the buyer that the business is solid, your employees hardworking, and your customers loyal. Never, never, never stop selling. Sell hard and be honest — but don't oversell or you will get caught by your boasts and exaggerations. **Building trust is the key element to the successful sale of a troubled business.** Don't tell the potential buyer that revenues will "double in the next year." They won't believe you and it will place your entire credibility at issue. Give the buyer a story that makes sense and which they can go home and tell their spouse about.

Let the Seller Beware: Evaluating Potential Investors and Purchasers

Common practice is to regard due diligence as only about the seller — this is **wrong**. If the sale involves payments over time or the assumption of obligations, you need particularly to know more about the buyer. Spending a morning in the local courthouse can answer many questions about a purchaser, including a history of prior litigation, PPSA, and tax liabilities.

There are many elements involved in evaluating potential investors and purchasers. The types of questions that you would ask of a competitor wanting to increase their market share are not the same as those you would ask of an individual with a

$10,000,000 inheritance who wants to purchase a business. Below are detailed the more important questions to consider when evaluating potential buyers.

Questions for Evaluating Buyers

- Can they afford it?
- How will they finance it (cash, loan, mortgage, or leverage)?
- Why are they investing (strategic or financial)?
- Do they need bank, small business association, or other approvals?
- What do they want (assets, franchise, customers, employees)?
- Timing: how quickly can they close?

W A R N I N G

After you determine the assets the buyer desires, guard them carefully. If they value your management, be prepared that if the sale falls through they will try to hire away your managers.

Can They Afford It?   The first question you need to answer about any potential buyer is, "Can they afford the price (i.e., is it worth your while to continue a dialogue with them)?"

Unfortunately, it can sometimes take several meetings to determine exactly what is being purchased and what the price is. To avoid wasting time with candidates who cannot afford the investment, early in the sales process and usually at the end of the first meeting, ask the candidate how they intend to finance the investment. Don't be shy. Tell them that you are very interested in going forward, but that you need some proof that they have adequate financial backing, at least within the range necessary to consummate a transaction.

How Will They Finance It (Cash, Loan, Mortgage, or Leverage)?   Many a seller has been surprised when at the end of the due-diligence period unforseen delays or new terms and conditions appear, dictated by a "lender," and the buyer informs the seller that the transaction is still subject to the buyer receiving adequate financing. If the transaction involves a loan or a mortgage on existing or to be acquired real estate or property, verify that the buyer has approval or at least determine how long the process will take.

If the deal is for all cash, then ask for some proof that the investor has the magnitude of cash available to them for this type of transaction.

As the seller, the types of financing to be most careful about are those where the buyer intends to leverage (borrow against) your company's assets or future cash flow to pay for the business. Although this is commonly done with larger LBO (leveraged buyout) transactions, with smaller and medium-sized businesses the transaction can get very sticky with a payment schedule that stretches over a time period.

Should a payment schedule over time be part of the payment terms, then you need to perform due diligence very carefully upon the purchaser. You are relying on their assets and good business judgement to secure your future payment stream.

Why Are They Investing (Strategic or Financial)? Investors can be divided into categories based on the reason they are making the investment.

Strategic players are those that are already in the business, or a related business, or desire to enter your marketplace and are making the investment for particular business reasons, not all of which are financial. Strategic players are usually patient and are willing to build or rebuild a business in the short run for a financial return in the longer term.

Financial players are interested strictly in receiving an economic return on their investment in some limited period of time. The period of time for their investment can be from a few months to a few years, but it is generally not a long-term investment unless your company has plans for making a public stock offering.

WARNING

Be wary of wolves dressed in sheep's clothing. Financial players may approach you dressed as strategic investors and strategic investors may tell you their only interest is a financial return. Both of these actors can cause you to play your role incorrectly and to ask the wrong questions. Examining a potential investor's past track record is a reasonably good predictor of their future performance.

Do They Need Bank or Other Approvals?   Don't wait until a few days before closing to discover that your potential buyer needs to have the investment approved by his board of directors, or his bank, or his franchisor before he can proceed. In some industries, regulatory approval, even in pro forma, may be required. Investigate early what approvals will be required on the buyer's side, you already know what approvals are necessary on the seller's side.

What Do They Need?   This question should more aptly be put as, "What do they **really** want?" If this is a strategic investment, then the investors may really be interested not in your company, but in one or more of your select assets. These objects of desire can include your real estate, your franchise rights, your exclusive on a particular territory or marketplace, your regulatory license to operate, your customer base, your employees, or your managers.

W A R N I N G

Once you have determined what assets you possess that are of strategic importance to the potential investor, guard these assets dearly. If the investor is most interested in your senior management, be prepared that if the plans for investment fail, he will try to acquire members of your senior management team without acquiring your company.

How Quickly Can They Close?   How quickly do you need to close? Do you have six months (not likely if you are reading this book), 30 days, 60 days, or 90 days? Don't sound desperate, but if you absolutely must have a commitment and a closed deal (i.e., cheque in hand) within the following 30 days, then tell the potential investor.

Moving to a Commitment

Most investors are either in a rush saying, "Only have today and tomorrow to examine the deal...," or they are interested but say, "We won't be able to get back to you for six weeks...." As the seller, you need to control the process. Tell the buyer when you expect a commitment and when you need to close. If they are interested, they'll find a way to accommodate your needs and if not, then as a troubled business, you shouldn't be talking to them.

Many engagements fall apart before reaching the altar. Last-minute jitters are more common in a business union than in a marriage. The key to a successful sale is to maintain good communications with your suitors — talk to them regularly.

Most importantly, **do not let outside advisors push the process into a breakup.** Lawyers are notorious for making ultimatums and absolute conditions and causing otherwise eligible and compatible suitors to become adversaries.

TYPES OF SALES

The type of sale that can be arranged is dependent upon the financial condition of the buyer and the seller, the assets that are being sold, the condition of the assets (i.e., are they being used as security for financial obligations), and the need for the principals to remain involved with the business.

Selling the Corporation

The simplest, though riskiest, transaction is the sale of the company's shares. By purchasing the corporation, a buyer inherits all of its obligations, debts, and history. With troubled businesses these unknown liabilities can include past-due taxes, penalties, pending litigation, accounts payable, leasing obligations, and employee benefits. If these liabilities are significant or unknown, the buyer may still be interested in the business, but not the corporation. Selling the business without the corporation is called a "bulk asset sale."

Although some assets can be obtained without purchasing the corporation, many may not be separable or transferable. If the business has assets such as franchise rights, service contracts, employment agreements, patents, favourable leases, or real estate, then it may be necessary to sell the corporation and all that goes along with the legal entity. **Seek professional advice on selling the corporation vs. selling only selected assets.**

Bulk Asset Sales

Provincial laws governing debtor and creditor relations vary, but disposing of significant assets beyond what would be considered ordinary business is generally prohibited, unless public notice is given to your creditors. Although these statutes were enacted to prevent a business from selling major assets without concern for its creditors, this doesn't mean you are required to telephone each of your creditors and remind them you have found a buyer.

Sales from Bankruptcy

A company that has filed for bankruptcy can still be sold. Don't file for bankruptcy to make it easier to sell the company, but neither should you give up hope of selling after filing. More than one company has discovered that after filing a bidding war developed, which raised the sale price. Sales from bankruptcy are a special art and should only be handled by an experienced lawyer.

What Happens to Your Employees?

It is difficult to guarantee jobs for all of your employees. Don't make promises that you will be unable to keep. The decisions about employees will be made by the new owners, not the former owners. Let them be the bad guys.

Most employees don't care who owns their company; it's just a question of who is their direct manager and their future prospects for compensation, benefits, and career advancement. If specific employees are an integral part of your business, you may want to work with the potential purchaser to negotiate employment contracts for these employees to secure their services.

These agreements can result in win-win-win situations. The employee benefits by knowing they will receive a salary and usually a bonus; the purchaser benefits from knowing they have secured the loyal services of an important employee; and the seller benefits from having overcome one of the obstacles to consummating a sale.

CLOSINGS

Less ominous than it sounds, a "closing" is simply the meeting of the parties (or their designated representatives) to finalize and consummate the transaction. Any adjustments to the price, terms, and agreements are made at the closing. The easiest way to have a successful closing is to be prepared: agree in advance on the documents that need to be exchanged and executed; be certain both buyer and seller have the opportunity to review the agreements; and plan for contingencies.

> **IT TAKES COURAGE FOR AN ENTREPRENEUR TO SELL THEIR BUSINESS**
>
> Although selling will not leave you as an independent owner, it may relieve you of the threat of economic ruin and it will allow you to go forward and start your next business. The keys to a successful sale are: proper planning, good marketing, and a positive attitude.

CHAPTER 11

˙IMAGE
AND
COMMUNICATIONS

COMMUNICATE WITH YOUR EMPLOYEES

Your company is a team, or at least it should function as one. As the team's quarterback, you need to inform the team members about the current predicament of the company and what is required of each of them to win the game. You don't have to make the playoffs or the Stanley Cup finals, but you don't want to place last in your league either.

When discussing the company's current situation with other managers and employees, don't hide the seriousness of the situation, but don't scare them with draconian predictions either.

Too often managers are observed trying to hide the major problems of the company from their staff until it is too late for the employees to work together as a team to gain any yardage on the field. Remember that no one likes to be surprised with adverse news.

Do not wait until the last minute to tell your staff that the company is experiencing troubles. Schedule a meeting or a series of meetings with your employees. Prepare yourself for the meeting — be positive, limit the surprises, and avoid attributing individual blame for the troubles. There is no advantage to be gained in blaming any one event, or one person, for the firm's current troubles. Excepting corporate responsibility for torts such as hazardous waste, medical products, foodstuffs, and product liabilities, it is rare that any one event can force a company into a situation of economic peril.

When meeting with your staff, be truthful and positive. It is appropriate to discuss the decline in the sales of your products and the high cost of operating the sales offices. However, it is inappropriate and imprudent of a good manager to tell a group of employees that, unless the situation improves, by the end of the month only half of them will have positions. It is also inappropriate to blame the troubles on the recently departed Vice President of Sales, or the "lousy" computer system.

Tailor your presentation to the level of the employee; be direct and be clear about your objectives. Tell them what your role will be during the coming months and what each of them can do to help the company to survive and prosper.

Even in the shadow of a series of business defeats always try to impart a positive and optimistic image. You are the leader and the team will rally around you. With proper motivation the team may take the ball further than you expect.

HOW TO TELL THE STAFF ABOUT THE COMPANY'S TROUBLES

1. Schedule the meeting for a morning in the early part of the week.
2. Provide doughnuts and coffee to set the stage for a friendly meeting.
3. Be prepared with an agenda — this is not an ad hoc meeting.
4. Remember to:
   • be positive;
   • tailor your presentation to the level of the employee;
   • be direct and be clear about your objectives;
   • limit the surprises;
   • avoid attributing individual blame for the troubles;
   • don't hide the seriousness of the situation;
   • don't make draconian predictions.
5. Tell them:
   • briefly how the company came to be in this position;
   • what the company's game plan is for recovery;
   • what your role will be;
   • what **each** of them can contribute to help the company meet its objectives.

6. Emphasize what you expect from each of them.

7. Assure them that there is a light at the end of the tunnel.

8. Ask them for their input and **listen** to them.

PUBLIC RELATIONS

Public relations (PR) is the external image that your company projects to the public. The company's external image may not resemble the true state of your company, it is the "perceived" truth about your company and its management. This image is more important during a troubled period than at any other time of your business history. **Do not ignore public relations.**

When experiencing financial troubles, expect that the world around you probably perceives your problems as even worse than they are. When laying off employees, expect that the public will think the company is on the verge of closing down all operations. When closing one or more locations, expect that the public will believe that the company is about to lay off all employees and terminate operations.

Managing PR is easy if the company plans for it. Public relations is almost impossible to manage if the company ignores it until a negative event happens.

Divide the public into three groups: customers, suppliers, and the media. Each group is important and the company will need a different strategy for managing public relations with each.

COMMUNICATIONS IN TROUBLED TIMES

- The worst attitude to take is to become introverted and like an ostrich, burying your head in the ground to hide from the world.

- During troubled times you may often feel like saying, "Help! Stop the world — I want to get off." At all costs you must fight on.

- The survival of your business depends on your ability to keep your head when times get tough.

Customers

Customers are the company's lifeblood and are responsible for furnishing it with a regular cash flow. Customers pay your salary and the company's rent. It is very important to **keep them happy.** List the company's 10 or 20 most important customers. Telephone each of them and arrange to have lunch or to meet with them during the next few weeks.

If these customers see you in the flesh and hear from you, they will be more likely to maintain a relationship with you. Be honest with your customers. Don't pour out all of the company's troubles on the table, but let them know that you are experiencing difficulties. Work on getting the customers to believe that the company will be in business for many years to come.

Evaluate your customers carefully, but don't mistake them for your friends. Customers are in business to make money. They may be sympathetic to the company's plight, but they are more likely to do business with a winner than with someone who may be a loser. Assure them that the company is committed to winning.

Ask customers about their business. Let them tell you their plans for the future and ally yourself with their plans. How can they not have confidence in a business person that has such a strong interest in their future?

Listen to your customers' concerns about your business. Why do they perceive the company as valuable to their future? How could the company provide better service? If you were to meet with them for lunch every month or two, to review business, would it be helpful to them? Recognize your weaknesses, be appreciative of any criticism offered, and ally yourself with the value that the customer perceives in your business.

This is not the occasion to break new ground or to plant new seeds. Don't push too hard for new sales from current customers. The objective of your lunch date is to maintain the customer's confidence and convince them of your ability to remain a viable partner in their business.

Near the holiday season, or on the anniversary of your starting the business or some other date of significance, it is beneficial to your public image to send greeting cards to your customers. Tell your customers you love them and add a personal note to as many cards as you can. If you can afford it, send small gifts to your customers as a token of your appreciation. Be conservative, not flashy. Nuts, candy, or fruit baskets are usually appreciated.

Don't forget to send thank you letters for renewals and new orders. These are the simple ways that you can use to let the customer know that their business is important to you. In a competitive marketplace, the personal approach may make the difference in maintaining a customer's loyalty **and their patronage.**

Suppliers

Relationships with suppliers are just as important as relationships with customers. Without products you will have nothing to sell.

But suppliers don't just sell you a product. They can also extend credit, speed up the delivery of special orders, accept returns, assist in disposing of excess inventory, and refer new customers. A good relationship with a supplier can stretch the company's cash flow, and a poor relationship can put it out of business.

The first rule in managing relationships with suppliers is not to surprise them. Don't promise them payment when you know the company can't meet the commitment. If the company can't make an expected payment, then communicate, be reasonable, and negotiate with the supplier.

The Media

The media will ignore the company unless something catastrophic happens. It is good practice to have some contacts in the trade and local media. You don't want your layoff of 20 employees to be your first notice in the local press. Start today to have a positive presence in the media.

What Works

Press releases work. Simple succinct notices sent to the local and industry press announcing good news about your company will be read and noticed. Issue press releases for upcoming events, new sales, big contracts, speaking engagements, awards received, promotions, expansions, and anniversaries. For speed, use a fax machine to distribute announcements to the media.

If you are contacted by the media for your comments on a news item, insist that any comments printed are attributed to you and printed verbatim. Many reporters write articles based entirely on an interview with one person, without giving them credit. An inquiring reporter should be told that you are willing to speak with them if you receive credit. If they refuse, tell them you are not interested.

When you receive recognition in the press, write the reporter and the editor and thank them. Let the media know whom they can contact for any questions about your company in the future. Send them a full media kit about your company for their files.

When your company receives recognition in the press, order professional reprints from the publisher. If you have camera-ready artwork, you can usually request these reprints with your logo, name, address, and telephone number on them. Send a copy of the reprint to every present, former, and potential future customer and to the company's suppliers.

What Doesn't Work

Don't treat reporters and editors to a free lunch or a drink — it usually doesn't work. If the news about your company is significant enough they will cover the story. If it isn't, a free lunch won't make a difference.

Be Prepared for the Media

Whatever happens, do not be caught unprepared for the media. You do not want to be in response mode when the media calls. You want to initiate the contact or be ready to respond on a professional level.

Have a media response plan for your company ready. Who is the designated person for responding to media inquiries? All media contact should be centralized. Inform all managers and significant employees in writing that it is company policy that all media contact must be managed and directed by the media contact person.

Assembling a Media Kit

Prepare a media kit and have several assembled and ready to be sent out at any time. The media kit should look professional. If you don't have the facilities for assembling the kit professionally inhouse, take the materials to your local copy shop and have them do it. The completed package should be presented in a folder with your company name on the cover and file pockets containing the inserts.

When building a media kit, the following is a list of inserts that are required and others that are optional.

CONTENTS OF A MEDIA KIT	REQUIRED	OPTIONAL
Company mission statement	✓	
Brief description of company	✓	
History of company	✓	
List of principals		✓
Business cards of principals	✓	
Biographies of significant principals		✓
Your media contact w/home tel. no.	✓	
Photographs of significant principals		✓
Photographs of major products or descriptions of services or locations		✓
Press releases (last 2 yrs)	✓	
Copies of product brochures	✓	

Update your media kit every few months and include inserts for new appearances in the press, new significant employees, and new products.

MAINTAINING IMAGE WHILE LAYING OFF EMPLOYEES

Its all a question of how you inform the world about the layoffs. Most medium-sized firms try to avoid publicity when forced to undergo layoffs, closings, or restructuring. Sometimes keeping a low profile will work. If the company is publicly-held, or is significant to the local community, or the industry, then you probably can't hide.

The following are a few examples of how other firms have presented layoffs to the media along with an analysis of the message the firm was trying to convey to the public.

Eckerd Drugs
"... reduced overhead expenses and fewer layers of management will translate into better customer service at competitive prices."[1]

(This means: layoffs will mean better customer service.)

Safeway Supermarkets

"We are committed to serving our customers well while having a much leaner administrative staff."[2]

(This means: layoffs won't affect customer service.)

John Fluke Mfg. Co. Inc.

"The streamlining [layoffs and closings] strengthens Fluke by letting it focus on its mission to be the leader in compact professional electronic test tools."[3]

(This means: without layoffs we can't provide better products.)

Lockheed Aeronautical Systems Co.

"We have been working hard to reduce overhead costs for a number of years. However, we must take this action to protect the well-being of our company....factors occurring over the past few months have contributed to the need for cutbacks, despite an ongoing, aggressive program to reduce costs....we cannot remain competitive if we don't take some decisive, timely appropriate action....the challenges [i.e., layoffs] facing Lockheed are the same industrywide."[4]

(This means: it's getting worse; without layoffs we will fail and anyway, everyone is doing it.)

Carefully consider the image that you want to project and give clear reasons for personnel cutbacks. Be honest in your reasons, but be selective in your announcements. "Consolidation" is a better word than "closing" and saying "economic pressure" is preferable to "our bank gave us no choice."

Even if you don't issue a formal press release, writing a draft of an announcement and distributing it internally will help all managers to project the "party line" and the correct image.

MAINTAINING IMAGE WHILE CLOSING LOCATIONS

Most entrepreneurs are loath to close a location because they believe the image presented is one of failure. The closing of a location is a project that requires careful handling to maintain the desired public relations image.

Customer Relations   If you are closing a retail location, don't neglect to inform your customers that you are "consolidating to provide better service...." Place a sign in the store informing the customers of the new location with as much advance warning as possible. Distribute cards with the new address and a map of the new location. Use the reverse side of the card for a discount coupon to entice the customer to visit the new location. Mail a copy of the card to all customers and suppliers. You are not closing the business, just closing a location.

Avoid New Telephone Numbers   If the company can afford the costs, ask the local telephone company to install automatic call forwarding service on the old number and have calls automatically transferred to the new location. If the company has multiple lines, request this service only for the primary voice number. Ask the local telephone company to terminate the other voice numbers and facsimile numbers and have a recording installed stating the equivalent telephone numbers at the new location.

Media Announcements   The local media may or may not take notice of a closing. This usually depends on whether there is more significant news that week. It may be to the advantage of the company's public image to send a brief press release to the local media informing them of the company's decision, with the appropriate reasons to maintain a positive image.

Press Release Announcing a Closing

The following is an example of a press release that announces the closing of two unprofitable locations of a laundry and dry-cleaning firm and maintains a positive image.

The press release maintains a positive image by calling the closing a "consolidation," and it headlines the closing by announcing the expansion of facilities at the main (and now the only) location. The business has done little "expansion" to the main facility, except for relocating two counter clerks from the locations to be closed in order to handle the additional volume, but the press release is entirely truthful.

The impression that is left with the reader is not one of a troubled business, but of a business undergoing **expansion** to provide **improved service**.

EXHIBIT 11-1

PRESS RELEASE

JOE'S DRY CLEANERS EXPANDS FACILITIES

FEBRUARY 22, 199-

Vancouver, British Columbia: Joe's Dry Cleaners, which has been providing quality dry cleaning and laundry services to North Vancouver for over 25 years, is proud to announce they are expanding their main plant and consolidating two satellite locations.

The newly expanded facilities will handle an increased volume of dry cleaning and provide faster turn-around service for customers. All business of the two locations to be consolidated will now be handled by the main store located at 123 Main Street, beside the car dealership. The enlarged store will be open from 7:00 a.m. to 7:00 p.m. Monday through Saturday to provide full customer service. Joe's telephone number will remain the same as always, 77-CLEAN.

The expansion and consolidation will be completed on Friday, March 4, 199-. All cleaning and laundry from the satellite locations will be available at the Main Street location on Saturday morning, March 5th.

Joe's want to thank all of their customers for the many years of business and welcomes all of them to visit the newly improved facilities.

For further information please contact Joseph or Julie Kaplan, at 77-CLEAN.

NOTES

[1]*St. Petersburg Times*, August 5, 1992, p.1-E, "Eckerd to eliminate 600 jobs," Helen Huntley.

[2]*Supermarket News*, March 8, 1993, "250 Positions eliminated as Safeway restructures," Elliot Zweibach.

[3]*The Seattle Times*, November 20, 1992, p.D-9, "Fluke to re-structure operations," Karen Alexander.

[4]*PR Newswire*, November 5, 1992, "Business changes force Lockheed to lay off 500," quoting Lockheed president, Ken Cannestra. Source: Lockheed Aeronautical Systems Company, Marietta, GA.

CHAPTER 12

WHO CAN
ASSIST
YOU

OUTSIDE ASSISTANCE FROM PROFESSIONALS

During troubled times business owners and principals will often go to great lengths to stay alive. Their actions are not always prudent. They will clutch at straws, mortgage their future, take counsel from pretenders and refuse counsel from sages. Who can forget automobile manufacturer John DeLorean's involvement with a cocaine deal, not to use the profits for his own personal benefit, but to keep afloat the automobile company that bore his name.

The cast of characters that will descend upon a troubled company is a motley crew of financial players/vultures: loan brokers, middle-men, "one-percenters," opportunists, and creative financiers. Most of these players are opportunists and very few have ever successfully helped a company in trouble. Mostly what they will do is raise your hopes and waste your time, and if you are foolish enough to pay their "expenses," they'll spend your money, too.

These birds of prey can carry business cards of reputable firms, but they will explain to you that your type of deal is one that they "need to handle on the side...," or that "they can't handle it, but they have a friend who for 1% can arrange an introduction...." Some of these birds are convicted felons, con-artists, and confidence men. Most work out of the front seat of their car or another person's office. Don't waste your time on them.

One simple way to sift the wheat from the chaff is to ask all "professionals" for references from businesses that they have "assisted" in the past year. Most of these "experienced" intermediaries and consultants are unable to provide any references. If they do give you names, then carefully check their references and maybe, just maybe, you have found a person who can help you.

There are those whose advice you may want to consider and those that you will have to consider. As a troubled company you may need legal, accounting, and consulting expertise as travelling companions on the road to recovery.

Lawyers

The troubled company will need legal assistance during the process of recovery, but be wary of using lawyers for business counsel. You wouldn't go to your dentist for advice on a sprained wrist, nor should you ask your legal counsel to be your business consultant.

You will need advice from a lawyer who has experience in very specific areas of the law. Most debtor/creditor relationships and remedies are governed by law; therefore, be certain that your counsel is well versed and experienced in debtor/creditor law in the primary location that you operate in.

A lawyer is only a good tool when utilized properly. Never forget that the lawyer is your servant — they work on your behalf. If a lawyer will not act upon your instructions, you may have to fire them.

Lawyers in small communities can easily have conflicts of interest when dealing with your creditors. If the lawyer, or their law firm, represents, or is under retainer to any of your creditors, they may be prohibited from representing you.

To make the process efficient, show the lawyer the list of your creditors and ask them if they have any conflicts of interest before discussing the merits and the details of your case.

Don't let your lawyer become an angry creditor. Work out a plan for the payment of their services. Avoid personally guaranteeing payment for the lawyer's services. All business is conducted with some amount of risk; lawyers would like you to believe that they conduct business without the same risk as your other vendors. This is not true and you shouldn't believe it.

Clearly document all instructions that you give to counsel. Confirm all telephone conversations in writing and fax copies to your counsel. Instruct your counsel that you **require** copies of all letters sent, court documents, pleadings, and memoranda sent or written on your company's behalf.

Trust your lawyer as a business associate with the role of providing legal counsel and advice. Never consider your lawyer to be your partner, because they are only your partner until you owe them money, then they can become your worst creditor.

See Chapter 14 on *Bankruptcy* for a detailed discussion of choosing counsel when contemplating the option of bankruptcy.

Accountants

Your current accountant may or may not be qualified to give you advice when facing economic troubles or possible insolvency. Many of the same rules that apply to legal counsel apply to accountants.

The accountant's code of ethics is much less strict than that of your legal counsel, and the information you or others in your firm impart to the accountant is not protected by the lawyer/client privilege. Do not confide in your accountant as you would in your lawyer.

If you need to choose a new accountant with expertise in insolvency and bankruptcy, then do so without hesitation. Nothing prevents a firm from having relationships with more than one firm of accountants. There is nothing wrong with using different tools to accomplish different tasks.

Many an accountant would like to play "lawyer" or management consultant, but you should be sceptical of those who try to wear too many hats. Some accountants are excellent management consultants, and some have more background and experience in the laws surrounding insolvency than your own lawyer. Listen to their ideas, but be wary of taking their advice before checking with your own legal counsel.

Turnaround Consultants

Consultants who bridge the gap between a company's management, creditors, lawyers, and accountants can be invaluable to the troubled company. Look for those that specialize in workouts, insolvency, business turnarounds, and debt restructuring.

Why You Need a Turnaround Consultant

Experience They are experienced at managing companies in a crisis. They know what to expect and will have solutions to the everyday problems of distressed companies.

Focus Their only job is the survival and resurrection of your business.

Time Even if you were able to make all of the correct decisions in a turnaround, you are unlikely to be able to do it and simultaneously manage the company.

New Blood Creditors will listen to experts who have successfully effected other workouts and arranged satisfactory payouts for creditors.

Contacts They know the best lawyers and accountants for assisting with a successful turnaround.

Unlike accountants and lawyers, they are not bound by any formal code of ethics. This can be an advantage. However, remember that nothing you tell the consultant is protected by the lawyer/client privilege and this can be a disadvantage.

Fees Negotiate a fee structure with consultants that rewards them for their performance, without placing them on a precipice when advising you. Consultants should be paid on a per day or per week basis, with a bonus based on meeting specific objectives. Some contingent fee structure is recommended, but don't put the majority of their compensation out on the limb until you are 100% certain of the course you intend to take.

GENERAL RULES FOR MANAGING RELATIONSHIPS WITH PROFESSIONALS
(including accountants, lawyers, consultants, loan brokers, etc.)

1. Require that all professionals execute an engagement agreement which includes protection for confidentiality, nondisclosure, and noncircumvention before undertaking the assignment.

2. Use the professional only for their specialty, don't try to use a hammer to do the job of a screwdriver.

3. Be ever vigilant of, and conscious of, conflicts of interest.

4. Confirm all instructions and "understandings" in writing. Use your fax machine to confirm and to acknowledge meetings and telephone calls.

5. Keep copies of all documents and correspondence sent to professionals. Stamp dates and times on all documents.

6. Don't permit the professional to become an angry creditor. They know too much about your business and could mortally wound you with their "inside" knowledge.

7. Know their code of ethics. Most will ignore it — you should not.

8. They are not your friend. They are in business to make a profit. They will only remain "sympathetic" as long as you are paying for their services. It's cheaper to use a psychiatrist than a business professional for a shoulder to cry upon.

9. Do question their invoices. Insist upon detailed billing, It may help to keep them honest.

10. Negotiate a fee structure in advance. Include a bonus or contingent fee, where appropriate and permitted.

CHAPTER 13

SECURITY AND THE TROUBLED COMPANY

INCREASE SECURITY TO CONTROL LOSSES

Although security should always be an important concern for management, a troubled firm must be extra careful to avoid any significant losses of material assets or information. Security breaches such as theft, fraud, and leaks of confidential information that are merely harmful to a healthy company can be fatal to the troubled company.

Many experts believe that corporate North America remains oblivious to the real depth of the problem of security in the workplace;[1] a troubled company cannot afford to ignore this risk. Security problems are like cancers. If left undetected, they can grow and fester for years before becoming fatal to their host. Management is often naive when it comes to the area of security. Even when confronted with irrefutable evidence that other firms in their industry have been "ripped off" or compromised, management will repeatedly deny that it is happening to them.

A troubled company can use many techniques to safeguard its business and property from harm. Although nothing management can do will result in a 100% secure business, a program of increased security will reduce and control the losses. These savings can mean the difference between the success and failure of a turnaround mission.

Fraud

Embezzlement, fraud, and kickbacks cost North American businesses more than $27 billion last year, and some experts believe the figure is higher because most companies are too embarrassed to report internal wrongdoing or simply never see it.[2] Estimates of the cost of telecommunications fraud alone, in Canada, range from $100 million to as much as $1 billion, annually.

Theft

According to experts, the cost of theft to Canadian business, both retail and wholesale, ranges from a conservative estimate of $5 billion a year to a high of $10 billion. **No business can succeed when its assets are being stolen, least of all a troubled business.**

Particularly in a distressed company, where workers are insecure about jobs and their company's commitment to them, workplace ethics have been eroded. Employees rationalize thefts while still seeing themselves as the "good guys" and the employer as the "bad guy." Even when caught in the act, employees rationalize their behaviour with excuses of low pay and "everyone does it."[3]

Leaks of Confidential Information

Most incidents of corporate espionage go undetected, and even those that are detected are often sheltered from publicity. "It is really quite common," says Brian Lowry, a leading security expert. "Most executives feel this is something that happens in a movie or to someone else, and really it is happening on a regular basis to a large number of corporations." His firm, Acclaim, prosecutes thousands of files in Canadian small-claims courts each year.

All companies are potentially at risk of corporate spying, but high-technology companies, companies bringing new products to market, and those with highly regarded customers have the highest risk.

Security expert Peter Schweizer, in his recent book *Friendly Spies,* estimates North American companies lose $100 billion annually to industrial espionage.[4] This is more likely to happen in troubled companies as workers look to gain an edge in the search for future employment. Everyone from GM to IBM has been hurt by losses due to theft of corporate secrets.

THE EVIL THAT LURKS WITHIN

Although police experts have estimated that almost two-thirds of all crimes against businesses are committed by their own employees,[5] many companies are still loath to admit they have a problem. Management will go to great lengths to protect the business from external threats without addressing the potential and real threat that lurks within. **Only through education can the attitudes about crime in the workplace be changed.**

A Reluctance to Prosecute

Many firms that discover criminal activity are reluctant to prosecute because of their fear of adverse publicity and embarrassment.[6] The "embarrassment syndrome" can become systemic to a company and thwart management's efforts to prevent and control future security problems.

Employees don't want to "rat" on other employees. Managers don't want to report their observations of employee dishonesty to corporate executives, and the executives don't want to alarm directors and shareholders, etc. This philosophy of denying and obscuring the true magnitude of the problem persists into the annual reports of most publicly held companies.

When was the last time you heard a company publicly admit that they had a problem with crime? Instead of telling their shareholders they have a problem with theft, companies simply add a category to their financial statements, euphemistically called "shrinkage," to accommodate any unexplained changes (thefts) of inventory.[7]

Why You Should Prosecute Dishonest Employees

Saying that a certain amount of crime is "acceptable" is a myth that managers would like to hide behind. When a troubled company is laying off employees and reducing benefits, no amount of "shrinkage" or "slippage" is acceptable or should be permitted. It should not be a surprise, experts say, that thefts by employees will rise to the highest level that management is willing to accept.[8]

Employers must work with their employees, in a team effort, to combat crime. **The primary reason for pursuing convictions against perpetrators is the deterrent effect that it has upon others and the support that it provides to honest employees.**

What the Troubled Company Can Do about Crime

The methods for combatting crime are the same for healthy or troubled firms; the only difference is that where a healthy firm may be able to withstand a few battlefield defeats before eventually winning the war, a troubled firm may bleed to death for lack of staying power.

The troubled company's arsenal of weapons in the war against crime can be referred to as **E-P-C**:[9]

HOW TO IMPROVE SECURITY
EDUCATION
PREVENTION
CONTROL

Education

Employees must be educated that crimes against the company are hazardous to the company's financial health and are everyone's concern.

Employees should be instructed that only with their support and vigilance can the problem be controlled and eradicated.

Management must instil a policy of "zero tolerance" for illegal and criminal activity.

Prevention

Companies should implement a loss-prevention program and employees should be trained in methods for preventing thefts and the procedures to follow when thefts have been detected. **No employee should be in a job without proper security training for their position.**

Alarm systems, security guards, and surveillance cameras are tools to employ as deterrents to prevent thefts. But when these tools are used without adequate operational and security procedures they are ineffective to prevent or even detect theft.

Most managers have no formal training in security procedures and are amateurs at preventing theft. Although the objective of a loss prevention program is not to make managers into detectives, their level of awareness must be increased.

Control

Detecting or deterring theft is only one element in the process. Companies need to employ methods to control theft and minimize the financial impact of the loss. The three elements to control illegal activity are: (1) deterrence, (2) surveillance, and (3) operating procedures.

Deterrence   Solid walls and ceilings, deadbolts, locks on doors, fences, bars on the windows, and operational procedures are all ways of deterring (controlling) theft, once experts have determined the locations where it can occur. Although these methods will not prevent thefts, they can delay access and reduce the probability of a breach in security.

Surveillance   Another element in the control process are alarm systems and surveillance cameras that reveal, if not prevent, forced or illegal entries.

Operational Procedures   A chain is only as strong as its weakest link. **Most important to the survival of a business are the operational procedures in place to prevent and control illegal activities.** Businesses must review their business and pinpoint areas that need improved procedural controls to improve security.

Hiring security professionals to observe the company covertly and review procedures can be a worthwhile expenditure, even for the troubled company.

Operational procedures that must be reviewed include cash handling, bank deposits, customer and manufacturer returns, and inventory tagging and control. Pickup and delivery on loading docks and in shipping departments and mailrooms should also be checked.

Security Management

Each area of the business requires some form of security management. The type of security procedure, the urgency, and the methods employed will be determined by three factors: (1) the value of the potential loss to the company, (2) the origin of the problem, and (3) the motivation of the perpetrators.

Value to the company   Although a company should implement a "zero tolerance" policy for any theft, it may be impractical or not economically feasible to enforce this throughout all areas of the company. Carefully evaluate the value of the potential loss to the company. Does it concern assets that are insured? Assets that are not needed anyway? Are the amounts involved small? Are the losses material to the company's business? Are the values small but highly visible and, therefore, important to control as a precedent?

Origin of the problem Security problems can originate from employees inside the company or competitors or third parties outside the company. A well-planned set of security procedures should prevent and control problems originating from both internal and external perpetrators.

Motivation of the perpetrators Perpetrators of security problems can be divided into three categories based on their motivation: accidental, intentional, or malicious.

Accidental problems occur through no intentional acts and are without motive. These problems can include a loss by fire or earthquake, the breaking of a window, or the unintentional reformatting of a computer's hard disk.

Intentional problems include thefts of supplies and equipment, industrial espionage, and the sale of company information in exchange for money, promises of employment, or other forms of compensation. All intentional security problems originate with an economic motive.

Malicious problems are those originating from sources that do not necessarily have a primarily economic motive. Although occasionally politically motivated, these types of problems usually originate with disgruntled current and former employees or partners, angry creditors, or angry customers.

EXHIBIT 13-1

MOTIVATIONS FOR SECURITY PROBLEMS			
TYPES OF PROBLEMS	MOTIVATION		
	ACCIDENTAL	INTENTIONAL	MALICIOUS
Natural Disasters	✓		
Theft & Pilferage		✓	✓
Diversion of Assets (Fraud)		✓	
Confidential Leaks	✓	✓	✓
Property Destruction	✓	✓	✓
Sales of Information		✓	✓
Procedural Lapses	✓	✓	✓
Industrial Spying		✓	✓

CONFIDENTIAL INFORMATION

Ever wonder how your competitor knew what price to offer to get the contract? How come they always seem to know what your plans are? Don't be surprised if your competitor spends a few dollars on corporate espionage.

Both low and high technology provide easy sources for confidential information about your company. Telephones, computers, fax machines, recycled materials, and trash are all overflowing with confidential information about your business. Take precautions to safeguard information if you want to keep it confidential.[10]

Many executives whom we have cautioned on the confidential content of their trash have ignored our warnings. A decision stated that, once rubbish has been put out for collection, it ceases to be private property. The following are real-life examples of why you should be concerned about the contents of your trash.

Dennis Levine, convicted of insider trading for sharing confidential information with fellow convicted felon, Ivan Boesky, was a frequent "trash picker." He reportedly broke into the investment banking firm of Lazard Freres armed with a seating chart identifying where everyone sat so that he could target only the wastebaskets of those having confidential corporate takeover information.

Cosmetics giant, Avon Products Inc., was recently accused in court by competitor Mary Kay of digging through a trash bin to uncover trade secrets and confidential documents.[11]

Then there was the arrest of two private detectives caught removing rubbish bags from the home of a British company director of Williams Holdings, which was involved in a takeover battle for the electronics group Racal. The British press had a field day writing about American business and its practice of snuffling around in their competitors' trash.[12]

Have we convinced you that someone might go through your trash tonight, or might have done so in the past?

Can You Protect Confidential Materials?

Use the E-P-C methodology to minimize the risk of confidential material being discarded in the waste basket. **Educate** all employees that confidential material needs to be kept locked in desk drawers when not being used and not to make unnecessary copies of confidential printed information. Give employees the examples in this book, or take a field trip to your own dumpster and show them what you can find. Don't make employees paranoid, but educate them to be informed about the consequences of their actions. **Prevent and control** the loss of confidential information by purchasing a shredder and making it policy that all confidential information be shredded before being discarded.

DIVERSION OF COMPANY ASSETS

Beware of employees operating personal businesses from your facilities. Such businesses are usually not secrets. Senior management may not be aware of the businesses, but the lunch room chatter would reveal that several of your employees probably operate, or are a party to, another business for supplemental income.

Most of these outside businesses are not your concern, because they don't compete with your company or interfere with your employee's job performance. However, there are cases where an otherwise honest and hard-working employee has used their employer's facilities, supplies, contacts, and even the company's credit rating, to launch their own business.

At one troubled company, we were looking into the backlog of repairs in their electronics shop. The first morning of the assignment, we observed extensive use of the telephones in the shop for what appeared to be personal calls. After consulting with the shop manager, we had the telephone disabled.

The company appeared to have recurrent shortages of electronic tools and parts. We requested that the manager conduct an inventory of the shop. During the inventory, we observed one technician who kept running back and forth to the pay telephone. Our suspicion was that the employee was operating a personal business. The following week, the technician resigned.

Later that week, the company received several orders of parts from unknown suppliers all shipped to the technician c/o the company. **Not only had the technician been operating a business from within the electronics shop, but he had been using the credit of his employer as venture capital to start the business!**

What You Can Do

If an employee sets up a business related to yours and uses your facilities, your customers, and your time to operate the business for their own personal benefit, they are taking money out of your pocket. Don't delay. Investigate thoroughly, and if you are certain, then ask for the employee's resignation, effective immediately. Where the matter involves theft of company assets, then report it to the police and prosecute without further delay.

Make certain that your other employees know why the employee has left; otherwise the experience is likely to recur.

Remember what the experts say: thefts by employees will rise to the highest level that management is willing to accept.[13] Only if the company has a "zero tolerance" for employee theft will the problem have a chance of being controlled.

Use the E-P-C methodology to reduce the potential loss and control the thefts.

Educate managers and employees that commercial use of company facilities for purposes other than the company's business is theft and will not be tolerated. Increase the awareness of managers to look for the indicators of diversions of company assets, including:

- Employees who stay late and come to the office on weekends and yet don't appear to be caught up with their work;
- Employees who receive an excessive amount of telephone messages or personal mail;
- Employees who appear to be making unusual requests for office supplies or equipment;
- Employees who refuse to take vacations.

Prevent the problem from spreading by limiting access to the facilities after hours and by being vigilant in looking for theft of company assets.

Control the problem by prosecuting all offenders and implementing a "zero tolerance" policy for all theft.

We often discover employees typing resumes, job applications, or academic term papers for friends after hours using company word processors. Even if the employee charges the friend for the service, this is not the type of business that requires harsh action (unless done on company time). A reminder to the employee to be judicious in their use of company resources and not to let it interfere with company business or be done during company time is usually sufficient to limit the practice.

USING PRIVATE SECURITY FIRMS

Don't use outside security firms as replacements for proper security procedures, but retain them to help your company to do risk assessment and construct a plan for risk management. The plan should include recommendations on education, prevention, and control of security risks.

Private security firms can provide a variety of services to the troubled company including background checks, corporate security reviews, criminal investigations, and investigations into financial fraud, industrial problems, insurance fraud and machinery malfunctions. As well, other services include photography, polygraphs, premises surveillance, protection, risk assessment, risk management, security guards, surveillance, warranty fraud, and workers' compensation liability investigations.

What to Request

Get good references. It is useful if the security firm has experience in your industry, but it is not essential. It doesn't matter if the business is a furrier or a bookstore — a warehouse is a warehouse.

Establish clear and concise objectives for security consultants. Tell them what you want from them and have them make a proposal. Get competitive bids from several firms, and select the firm most responsive to your needs.

If you need to hire security guards, be certain that the firm trains all of their guards and has the resources necessary to manage them.

E-P-C REVIEWED

Managers should use a combination of education, prevention, and control to create a **secure environment** to conduct their business.

Stopping illegal activity isn't a matter of more expensive technology to scrutinize every activity in the business. Preventing and controlling illegal activity requires well-designed management practices, close management and employee cooperation, professional assistance and, most importantly, educational awareness of the problem.

Don't ignore the issue of security until after you suffer a loss. A troubled company can easily be mortally wounded by only one or two small losses.

Don't think that security is something that only healthy companies can afford. Good security is not expensive, but it does require a change in attitude and a regular program of education.

If you need to employ security professionals then don't hesitate. Since you probably can't afford the costs of the losses, you can't afford not to hire professionals to assist in designing a program of prevention and control.

Practice E-P-C every day and for every new project. Make a security risk assessment a requirement of every new project. The same way a budget is designed for every project, a security program must be incorporated.

NOTES

[1]*Information Week*, August 10, 1992, "Weak Links — For corporate spies, low-tech communications are easy marks."

[2]*U.S. News & World Report*, April 13, 1992, Vol.112, No.14, p.55, "Crime and the bottom line," Terri Thompson, David Hage, Robert F. Black.

[3]*Gannett News Service*, October 30, 1992, "Employee theft on the rise," Judith Egerton, *Louisville Courier Journal*, quoting Joe Mele, loss prevention specialist with the National Crime Prevention Institute at the University of Louisville in Louisville, Kentucky.

[4]*Friendly Spies*, Peter Schweizer, Atlantic Monthly Press, New York, 1993. This book is an excellent account of the depth of corporate espionage by French, Japanese, and Israeli interests, all aimed at gaining economic advantage over the United States. After reading this book, many corporate executives will be loath to leave their briefcase unattended while in a foreign country or to give a factory tour to a foreign "specialist."

[5]*The Seattle Times*, March 17, 1993, p.D-10, "Nordstrom hires firm to fight employee theft," Scott Williams.

[6]*The Plain Dealer*, February 24, 1993, p.3-G, "Loose lips could sink firm's profits; corporate espionage on rise," David Schwab.

[7]*Distribution*, November 1991, p.84, "How to cope with theft and drugs; warehouse theft and workplace," E.J. Muller.

[8]*Gannett News Service*, October 30, 1992, "Employee theft on the rise," Judith Egerton, *Louisville Courier Journal*.

[9]*Business Insurance*, December 14, 1992, p.19, "Ask a risk manager; holiday pressures spur violence in the workplace," Susan M. Werner.

[10]Although provincial laws governing trade secrets and federal laws governing electronic communications were enacted to protect the private company, most violations are not detected and the laws are difficult to enforce.

[11]*The National Law Journal*, April 1, 1991, p.43, "Cosmetic Litigation," Associated Press.

[12]*The Independent*, November 24, 1991. p.4, "Tricks of the trash trade: Garbage is fair game for US business spies," Edward Lucas.

[13]*Gannett News Service*, October 30, 1992, "Employee theft on the rise," Judith Egerton, *Louisville Courier Journal*.

BANKRUPTCY

WHAT IS BANKRUPTCY ALL ABOUT?

In December 1993, Remiera Corp. made a *Financial Post* list of the country's best-managed companies.

On January 17th, 1994 the wheels fell off at Remiera Corp. when a cheque for $400,000 from a network software development partner failed to arrive.

Remiera, an $8 million privately-held computer service company, sought bankruptcy protection on February 9th, 1994, with $2.6 million owed to creditors.

Fortunately for the company's 85 employees, on March 14th, 1994, AT&T reached an agreement with the trustee in bankruptcy, Ernst & Young Inc., and the lead secured creditor, The Royal Bank of Canada, to buy the assets of the company.

It is not nearly as simple as this for the 1,000 or more incorporated companies that go bankrupt every month in Canada.

The experiences for Silcorp, Algoma Steel, Curragh Mines, Central Guaranty Trust, and dozens of major Canadian retailers and real estate developers from Olympia and York to Trizec have been long drawn out and expensive, costing millions in legal, receiver, and accounting fees and in thousands of jobs.

One philosophical view of bankruptcy is that it keeps the debtor honest, or at least gives them a conscience of a sort. As Frank Borman, Apollo astronaut and former chairman of Eastern Airlines, said when the company went into bankruptcy while under his helm, "Capitalism without bankruptcy is like Christianity without hell." An alternative view was held by the actor Errol Flynn, who was perpetually in debt, who said, "Any man who has $10,000 left when he dies is a failure."

Bankruptcy, in its simplest form, allows a debtor, who petitions the Court, to be relieved of the obligation to pay all of those debts that are dischargeable under the Bankruptcy and Insolvency Act.

THE AMERICAN VERSUS CANADIAN VIEW

The provisions of the U.S. bankruptcy code as currently used go back to 1978, with the installation of the now famous Chapter 11 section of the code. This is widely used for delaying bankruptcy liquidations or major judgements from lawsuits and permits massive debt restructuring.

Even with the reform on November 30, 1992 of the 46-year-old Bankruptcy Act, in many ways the options available in each country were quite different, as was their culture basis.

The American orientation was more towards a second chance. Yet only 15% of Chapter 11 companies come out of it successfully. The United States, with its greater entrepreneurial orientation and focus on state and individual rights, developed its own approach, distinct from British common law and conservative banking.

American legislation allows the business, if it can afford it, to commence proceedings to aggressively protect its assets, and it provides more flexible options for liquidation and reorganization. In many cases, this has led to abuses and applications never intended by the legislators.

Yet Canada has a rate of business failure two-and-a-half times greater than the U.S., for reasons already mentioned. One would expect governments to be more attentive to the legislation. Yet six times since the 1940s amendments and new acts were proposed only to die on the order paper.

The Canadian view of bankruptcy draws its roots from our economic history. The Canadian business society, particularly banking, was developed and totally dominated from 1820 on by a small group of Scottish Calvinists who believed strongly in thrift and conservative practices, with a strong aversion to debt and borrowing.

There was an inherent need in the case of financial difficulty to act quickly to protect depositors' funds by liquidating a business and its assets and to pursue the borrower aggressively for personal assets and security.

The historical view was to liquidate. Now in the mid 1990s, it is to reorganize.

COMPANIES' CREDITORS ARRANGEMENT ACT

While the Companies' Creditors Arrangement Act was enacted in the "Dirty '30s," it was little used until the late 1980s. This act, a vague and unspecific piece of legislation that literally lets the lawyers and court fill in the blanks as they proceed, is actually not dissimilar in its intent with the U.S., Chapter 11 concept. But during its first 50 years of existence, it was rarely applied. Today, despite the new Bankruptcy and Insolvency Act, which parallels the Companies' Creditors Arrangement Act (CCAA), the old statute will be kept on the books for at least three years until November 30, 1995 so that we can experience the new act and make revisions.

It is perhaps a daily occurrence for us to receive a call that "X retailer" has gone "CCAA". Murray Page of Page Hill & Associates of Toronto, a 40-year practitioner in the field of bankruptcy, says, "The very existence of CCAA is to the principal benefit of solicitors, who make substantial fees from the process, and not to the benefit of public or creditors, or for that matter, the company itself."

The sheer vagueness of the CCAA legislation allows substantial freedom and negotiating opportunity, and it is far less rigidly controlled than the new Bankruptcy and Insolvency Act (BIA).

However, with an economy severely damaged by massive bankruptcies and job loss, the concept of CCAA or its new form in the BIA does have validity. The old CCAA does not impose deadlines and leaves most decisions to the court.

202 TURNAROUND: The Canadian Guide

In 1988, insolvency meant 80% of the businesses in difficulty were pushed into liquidation and 20% into reorganization and turnaround. In 1994, the view is to save 80% and liquidate 20%. The turnaround is the thing, if at all possible.

Because of the failure of the prior Bankruptcy Act to provide management with a mechanism of flexibility, CCAA has become a major instrument and source of power in dealing with creditors. If the CCAA plan is rejected, then creditors could still petition the company into bankruptcy and liquidation.

Limitations of CCAA

The major drawback of CCAA is that it is quickly recommended by solicitors before management has thoroughly contemplated its implications. Working capital is required to run the business and pay the substantial legal fees during the process.

Critics also argue that this type of restructuring is too often used by management and directors as a means to retain their jobs and salaries as long as possible.

According to Ed Waitzer, formerly of Stikeman Elliott and currently chair of the Ontario Securities Commission, the act is biased towards reorganization. This is not always the best or most logical alternative for creditors or even in the best interest of the company.

The Bankruptcy Act Prior to November 30, 1992

Under the old act, a company could reorganize itself by filing a proposal which, when approved by the requisite number of creditors (secured), allowed it to stave off its unsecured creditors. These unsecured creditors simply had no remedy or course of action while the company was allowed to reorganize itself.

The so-called "protection" under the act did not apply to secured creditors, who were free to appoint a receiver or move to liquidate assets to service their claims. The process simply handed control of the business from management to secured creditors.

Benefits of CCAA

Under CCAA filings, this stage of proceedings prohibits all creditors from acting without court approval. Therefore, the control is in the hands of management and judge.

The CCAA statute is a simple and brief one. It describes the process under which a company must operate to secure CCAA protection, and it gives a definition of classes of creditors and voting regulations for creditors.

The CCAA provides no timing guidelines for reorganization and fails to explain the scope of the stay, the rights of landlords, and how creditors can be classified.

The opportunity to utilize the act is handed to the court and opposing legal counsel. This can result in high fees to lawyers and the need for cash flow to pay the bills.

The vagueness of the process and the fact that the act was allowed to be used unmodified since the 1930s resulted in court decisions generally favourable to business management. The court's general view is that the purpose of the act is to permit a business to operate, despite its financial insolvency, in order that the business be allowed to be reorganized.

The courts have restricted the rights of creditors to cut off services, from utilities to principal suppliers, as they may be deemed to be essential to the company's survival under its plan.

The CCAA has been treated with great flexibility to ensure that companies have both the time and legal clout to negotiate a reasonable settlement with creditors and ensure some fairness on both sides.

The *Canadian Investment Review* cites the case of Campeau Corporation, which was insolvent as a result of its acquisitions of Federated and Allied stores.

It applied for protection under CCAA, with the following results:

- Debentures, unsecured debt obligations, and outstanding common shares were exchanged for a new class of common shares;
- All outstanding rights, options and warrants to acquire shares being cancelled;
- Officers, directors, executives, and advisors being released of all claims and liabilities from shareholders and unsecured creditors;
- The real estate assets of the company being transferred to a new company, Camden Properties, which was allowed to assume the secured indebtedness against the property.

The CCAA Process

- The company's financial debts must be secured or issued under a trust deed.
- The trust deed can be created on the day of the filing.

- The company applies to the court for protection from its creditors to permit time to create the reorganization plan.
- The court classifies creditors for evaluation. The only separate classes are secured or unsecured.
- The company negotiates with creditors as to creditor classes and treatment under the reorganization plan.
- The plan is developed and presented to each group of creditors for approval. If each group approves, the court sanctions the plan and its finding on all parties.
- There is minimum court supervision and no administrative control.
- A monitor is selected, with broad authority, to observe and report on progress.
- The company, its lawyers, and creditors negotiate settlements usually lasting from six months to two years, with substantial professional fees. There may be ongoing court motions, appeals and legislation.
- The cooperation of the operating lenders must be secured, as will the support of the majority of creditors.
- Major secured creditors must agree to the plan and support it or the court will allow a petition into bankruptcy.
- The discipline of the process is the cash resources of the company and the willingness of the judge to allow the process to proceed.

Key Considerations

- Is the plan fair to all parties?
- Will the reorganization plan likely succeed?
- How can we minimize our costs? Can inside staff do some of the work, prepare the list of creditors, do the inventory and prepare much of the plan?
- Can management resolve agreements with landlords and suppliers without using legal assistance?
- Will the plan adversely affect the major relationship of directors?
- Is the solution reasonably consistent with what major secured creditors would get under a bankruptcy proceeding?
- Will the plan be approved by both classes of creditors? A majority of each class plus 15% of those voting is needed for approval.
- Is it fair to both classes of creditors?

- Will the critical operating lender stay in place, or can a new one be found to ensure the ongoing operation of the business?
- Will adequate management and directors stay in place to ensure the business will be run properly?

THE DIFFERENCES UNDER THE BANKRUPTCY AND INSOLVENCY ACT OF 1992

The new act shares many of the same objectives of the old CCAA. It is far more detailed and specific, reducing the potential for creativity and problem solving needed for a total reorganization. This probably means that the days of CCAA are numbered.

Under the Bankruptcy and Insolvency Act (BIA), both classes of creditors are prevented from acting against the company. The forms and procedures under BIA are quite specific and precise as to the reorganization time period. Every group's treatment is defined: landlords, employees, and the government.

How the bankrupt company is to finance itself and its reorganization process is not defined under BIA.

BIA does not close off the CCAA program, but be prepared for more courts to move to unite the features of both CCAA and BIA under one roof.

THE BANKRUPTCY AND INSOLVENCY ACT, AMENDED NOVEMBER 30, 1992

Commercial Restructuring   One of the most important amendments provides for an automatic 30-day restructuring period for companies in financial trouble and in need of protection from creditors while they renegotiate debts.

Under the new legislation, a firm in difficulty has two options after a 30-day restructuring period: it can present a commercial reorganization plan, or it can apply to the court for 45-day extensions of its stay in order to prepare a plan, up to a maximum of five months. A meeting of creditors must be held within 21 days after a commercial reorganization plan is filed. If unsecured creditors vote to reject the plan, the company is declared bankrupt. The new Act also protects the interests of creditors by enabling them to have stays lifted if their interests are in jeopardy.

Previous legislation allowed secured creditors to terminate agreements or demand accelerated payments which, the federal government says, forced "potentially viable enterprises into premature bankruptcy or receivership."

Within 21 days of filing the proposal, creditors must vote on the plan. If it is rejected, the company can apply for more time to work on its restructuring. However, if unsecured creditors do not accept the proposal, the company is automatically placed in bankruptcy.

Creditors also can apply to have stays lifted if their interests are in jeopardy, but the court is free to impose conditions if it decides to end the protection.

The new rules allow cash-strapped tenants to break commercial leases by paying a maximum six months' rent.

The new legislation was envisioned a few years ago when commercial rents were increasing and the landlord could easily rerent the premises. These new laws may have a disastrous effect on landlords in the current commercial real estate market.

Unpaid Suppliers   Unpaid suppliers have gained rights to reclaim goods that are identifiably theirs within 30 days of delivery to a firm that subsequently declares bankruptcy. Other than in Quebec, unpaid suppliers have not been able to recoup unpaid inventory.

Farmers, fisherman, and aquaculturalists get extra protection. They are allowed to make a priority claim on all inventory of a purchaser for goods supplied up to 15 days before a bankruptcy or receivership.

Role of Receivers   While trustees can no longer be held accountable for damages to the environment which existed prior to their appointment, receivers are inheriting new responsibilities.

Receivers have to give debtors 10 days' notice of their intention to recoup assets, which will give the debtor time to put a 30-day stay in place to reorganize operations.

Receivers have new responsibilities, including monitoring the financial performance of companies operating under protection from creditors. "They'll have to do a mini-audit, almost on a weekly basis."

While the new law should be of use to many struggling businesses, firms still have the option of using the CCAA, which doesn't impose as many deadlines and leaves more decisions to the courts.

Some of the egregious injustices in the old bankruptcy law have been corrected. For example, employees who lose their jobs in an insolvency are now preferred creditors with claims of up to $2,000 for back wages and vacation pay, rather than the former limit of $500.

The money, of course, has to be available. Ottawa dropped a plan to guarantee such payments through a worker-protection fund because it would have been too costly to finance.

Another major irritant to many creditors has been removed. The federal and provincial governments no longer stand first in line to collect what they're owed, except in the cases of unremitted income tax deductions, unemployment insurance premiums, and Canada Pension Plan contributions.

Special Protection for Unpaid Suppliers

The legislation gives broader protection to unpaid suppliers. Within 30 days of the delivery of goods to a firm that is subsequently declared bankrupt or in receivership, unpaid suppliers will have the right to reclaim goods that are clearly identifiable as theirs, are unaltered, and have not been sold to a third party.

The BIA also protects farmers, fishermen, and aquaculturists as suppliers of perishable commodities. They are able to make a first-priority claim on all the inventory of the purchaser for goods supplied up to 15 days before a bankruptcy or receivership. The claim must be filed within 30 days after the bankruptcy or receivership, and it is subject to the right of an unpaid supplier to reclaim goods under the 30-day provisions.

The Strategic Implications

The primary goal of considering either CCAA or BIA is to restructure and reorganize the business to maximize its chances for survival.

This is particularly important if you happen to be an owner/ manager or shareholder. This is not to say that management isn't equally committed to survival, but owners do have their "life" on the line and are therefore more in need of a survival plan.

To consider these financial reorganization options, the situation must be severe and the alternative chances of refinancing or a "white knight" are slim. But management must take the lead and not wait for creditors, banks, or government to react. To react reduces options and reduces planning time.

Repeatedly, we have seen situations where the bank initiated action and considered liquidation the only option, demonstrating their complete lack of understanding of the business and markets.

Banks do not want messy or troublesome files lying about. They appear to be willing to take a liquidation value of 10%-20% rather than work through the situation and recoup 100%.

Their bad loans departments are generally staffed by people who wish to clear out files, not manage them to their fullest potential. If these bankers were creative and entrepreneurial, they wouldn't be bankers, would they?

The case of C.C. Yacht and Druxy's Deli's and restaurants are all good illustrations. C.C. Yacht was progressing successfully in 1988, with record sales and inventory. It was the only Canadian large-yacht producer. The upper middle class, particularly doctors and other professionals, were buying more boats than ever.

However, they never counted on their friendly bank, where an account manager read a U.S. report of an impending downturn in yacht sales. He quickly called the demand loan without significant cause.

What are half-finished yachts or inventory worth when there are no other Canadian buyers? The bank was incorrect and, rather than permit adequate time for refinancing, they liquidated, taking a substantial loss without purpose.

A refinancing group was being organized and was formulating a proposal. The bank was not interested in waiting. All was lost, especially a Canadian market leader and a lot of jobs. (A group did step in and picked up some of the pieces.)

How could management protect itself? The answer is that whenever you are in a cyclical industry you must build strategic partnerships offshore in case of emergency, as well as constantly sourcing new sources and types of financing. Management never considered CCAA because the company was too small and in 1988 lawyers never saw it as an option.

Druxy's Deli is a chain of 50 delicatessens in Ontario with an innovative and successful menu. Founded in the 1970s, the company had grown to $40 million sales in all company-owned units.

Business was good but the company used its operating lines to build restaurants and by 1988 had created $15 million in debt, just as interest rates began to rise and the recession began inducing sales to fall. Needless to say, the bank became nervous and demanding. Demands were made. The company quickly searched for new financing and equity, which was not forthcoming for a restaurant chain.

The bank moved to foreclosure. It was aware that, at best, a restaurant in liquidation will yield 10¢ on the dollar. The bank could expect only $1.5 to $2 million on its loan, but they did not seem to care. Their goal was to clear the file and liquidate.

The company proposed a plan of franchise conversion, selling the restaurants as franchises, with multiple sales, and diverting the cash to the bank to discharge the debt. We were engaged to fight the bank to a standstill and design and implement the franchise plan. Over the next 18 months corporate overheads were cut as the company went from a restaurant operations-line organization to a franchised staff-managed system. Debt was reduced, much to the bank's chagrin, from $15 million to $2.5 million and a substantial profit was realized.

Neither case used the CCAA route, although it was possible. Larger real estate and major retailers have opted for it instead. Elements of Grafton Fraser Stores and Maher Shoes have been saved. Bargain Harold's was not so lucky.

Algoma Steel is more of an exception because 5,000 jobs in Sault Ste. Marie were involved and government participated. A sharp drop in the dollar, a fall in the cost of money with a decline in interest rates, the automotive industry boom and Dofasco's restructuring out of Algoma's line of steel have turned a total writeoff into a large profit and an enormous recovery in stock market price. None of these are normal conditions you can really count on to save your business.

Some Special Considerations of the BIA

The new act will force the banks to negotiate more as it will take them longer to take possession of their collateral. The new act increases your bargaining power with your landlord by threatening CCAA and particularly BIA.

BIA permits you to cancel leases with six months' payment, and will bring landlords with 40% vacancies in office towers, 20% in malls, and 30% in industrial space to the table to work out a deal.

Such negotiation will permit a more proactive approach for retailers, in particular permitting downsizing and restructuring before it is too late.

CCAA is now being aggressively used to reorganize companies by protecting primarily the shareholders, management, and secured creditors but leaving the unsecured trade suppliers and land-lords bearing the cost of the insolvency.

Companies are using CCAA as a strategic vehicle to strengthen and reorganize their balance sheets by eliminating a large portion of current liabilities. This is certainly the view of the Trade Indemnity Group in Ottawa, a major credit insurer.

The trade suppliers receive only a small portion of their receivable over a period of many years. The so-called dividend payout is rarely guaranteed and is only a cash flow or profit dependent commitment. Secured creditors will receive deben-tures, preferred shares, or convertible equity as part of their guaranteed compensation.

As a result, in order to remain competitive more retailers will move to CCAA to respond to what competitors are already doing. If one gets away with it others usually follow to remain competitive. Small retailers unable to finance a CCAA will be at the mercy of the larger ones who can.

Supplier Protection under BIA

Suppliers frequently fall prey to a form of financial abuse known as "juicing the trades." A failing business, facing receivership and a shortfall to the bank, may substantially increase its stock of inventory shortly before bankruptcy or receivership. The effect is to increase the bank's recovery under its security, thereby minimizing the guarantors' exposure for a shortfall, all at the expense of the trade suppliers.

While in extreme cases this conduct may amount to provable fraud, the suppliers usually have no remedy.

Certain producer industries are unusually vulnerable to insolvency. Farmers fall into this category, as they typically market the entire year's production in a small number of sales transactions. Frequently, the farmer sells the entire year's produc-tion to one buyer. Hence, if the buyer defaults, a substantial portion of the farmer's annual production is at stake. Farmers cannot con-trol the price they receive and cannot increase the price at year-end to compensate for bad debts. Because of their vulnerability, farmers have mounted a successful lobby for added protection.

Overview of Sections 81.1 and 81.2

Unpaid-supplier protection consists of two provisions. Section 81.1 permits suppliers to repossess their goods under specific conditions. This remedy is analogous to the right of revindication under articles 1543, 1998, and 1999 of the Quebec Civil Code, and the right of reclamation under 546(c) of the U.S. Bankruptcy Code and 2-702 of the U.S. Uniform Commercial Code.

Section 81.2, which was hastily tabled and approved by the Common's Standing Committee at the conclusion of its deliberations, creates an extra measure of protection for farmers, fishermen, and "aquaculturists" (those who cultivate aquatic plants and animals) by giving them a superpriority over inventory under certain conditions.

Section 81.1 — Right of Repossession

A supplier may repossess unpaid-for goods within 30 days of delivery to a business which has gone bankrupt or has been placed into receivership. The supplier must present a written demand for repossession within 30 days of delivery. Unless the purchaser, trustee, or receiver promptly pays the entire balance owing, it must allow the goods to be repossessed, provided that, at the time of the demand, the goods:

- are in the possession of the purchaser or its trustee or receiver;
- are identifiable;
- are in the same condition;
- have not been resold, or been subject to any agreement for sale, at arm's length.

The supplier's right of repossession ranks above all other statutory or common law claims to the goods, except that of a *bona fide* subsequent purchaser for value without notice of the repossession demand. The right does not preclude the supplier from resorting to any other rights under provincial law, save that a supplier who repossesses goods under s.81.1 is not entitled to be paid for those goods.

Where the goods have been partly paid for, the supplier has a choice. It may repossess a proportional portion of the goods relative to the unpaid amount, or it may repossess all of the goods on refunding the partial payments previously received.

Once the trustee or receiver has admitted in writing the validity of the claim for repossession, the supplier must retrieve the goods within 10 days, failing which the repossession right expires. This period may be extended on consent.

The right of repossession applies only in the event of bankruptcy or receivership. It is inapplicable to commercial proposals under the new act. The commencement of a proposal proceeding, however, suspends the running of the 30-day period, so that if the proposal is ultimately defeated or rejected by the court, unpaid suppliers may at that time have recourse to recover whichever of their goods remain identifiable, unsold, unaltered, and still in the debtor's possession.

Effect of Reorganization Proceedings

The government has conceded that, notwithstanding the political expediency of unpaid supplier protection, the protection should not stand in the way of reorganization proceedings under Part III. The success of any reorganization is dependent upon an effective stay of proceedings so as to maintain the status quo during the process. The exercise of unpaid suppliers' rights would defeat the status quo and dismember the company's asset base at the very time when maintaining its integrity is most essential.

In the original version of Bill C-22, the protection under s.81.1 was lost upon the commencement of a Part III commercial proposal proceeding, even if the proposal was ultimately rejected or defeated by the creditors. Since the automatic 30-day stay precludes the appointment of a receiver or the bankruptcy of the debtor within that time, the unpaid preproposal supplier would never have been able to fulfil the requirements of s.81.1 before the expiry of 30 days from delivery. The concept of relation back is inapplicable to s.81.1 in so far as it pertains to proposals.

The section was subsequently amended to add s.81.1(4), which suspends the running of the 30-day period upon the commencement of a proposal proceeding. Until the proposal is defeated, the debtor can use or dispose of the goods. However, if the proceeding is ultimately unsuccessful, the unpaid supplier may exercise its repossession rights against any remaining goods which, at that late date, are still identifiable, unsold, un-altered, and in the debtor's possession.

One can expect an increase in "tactical" proposals which, although doomed to defeat, are filed for the sole purpose of deferring and frustrating the unpaid suppliers' right of repossession. The principals of a business, facing an impending shortfall on the guaranteed bank debt, will bulk up on inventory and then file a proposal. Until the proposal has been defeated, they can sell off or utilize the inventory to reduce the bank debt. By the time the proposal has been defeated, much of the repossessable inventory will have been sold or altered, thus substantially eroding the reach of the suppliers' repossession rights.

THE OPTIMAL RESOLUTIONS UNDER BANKRUPTCY — WHAT'S BEST

The predominant rationale for bankruptcy reorganization law is to solve the collective action problem among creditors that prevents the preservation of the insolvent firm, although it is worth more as a going concern than as the sum of the value of its assets.

The Canadian Bankruptcy and Insolvency Act does not go as far as the U.S. Bankruptcy Code's Chapter 11 in permitting a long period of time for reorganization nor does it impose the degree of regulation prescribed in the U.S. Code.

The goal is to determine what is best for the shareholders and creditors in the longer term. The uneven distribution of assets and liquidation rarely produces satisfactory results. Management may act capriciously in the short term and force credits into inequitable situations, or management may act to use assets not in the best interest of shareholders as a means of cramming down creditors. The bankruptcy mechanism forces all parties into a standstill situation or stay of proceedings until a proper course of action can be determined to preserve surplus value.

If the going concern value exceeds the liquidation value, it is in the collective best interest for the business to be preserved.

The usual strategic options for an informal workout are:

- One creditor, shareholder, or third party investor makes an offer to buy out all the other parties;
- A group of creditors buys out the balance of the secured or unsecured debt and becomes the single creditor in a position to deal;
- The business as a going concern is put up for sale at auction so that market forces can determine the excess value over book;
- Instead of uniting the claims in one investor, an alternative solution is for the claimants to agree to trade their claims for new interests in the going concern. This restructuring plan includes new debentures, convertible preferreds, income debentures, and new equity to creditors.

The formal bankruptcy process provides two compulsory and collective systems:

1. Liquidation by a trustee of the assets to a third party with the proceeds distributed to creditors according to a set of priority rules;
2. Formal reorganization — a proposal for arrangement.

Fixed claims are traded for new claims and ownership interests in the young concern.

Research shows that:

*   For publicly held firms, a going-concern sale in bankruptcy to a third party is a more effective mechanism for saving the going-concern surplus than is formal reorganization. The costs of information, transactions, disputes, and valuation are less with a third party than with the formal judicial process;
*   Sale by auction of assets is less efficient in preserving going concern value than third-party sale;
*   Formal reorganizations last longer than informal workouts;
*   Formal reorganizations cost 10 times as much as private restructuring.

The BIA is designed so that:

*   There is a stay of individual enforcement rights;
*   There is a negotiation and confirmation procedure for reorganization proposals;
*   There are provisions that maximize and preserve the going-concern surplus of the business during reorganization;
*   There is a safekeeping mechanism that minimizes the strategic use of the process by ensuring that bankruptcy is only invoked where gains can be made by resolving conflicts among claimants.

The process elects a licensed trustee to monitor the affairs of the insolvent business. This permits creditors to apply to the court if they feel management is damaging their security.

Thus, the central role of bankruptcy law is to provide a compulsory collective proceeding in restructurings that disciplines creditors in restructurings who might hold out for larger shares of the going-concern surplus value of the business. Research clearly shows that avoiding the formality of the system is far preferred to the costly formal proceedings. Informal solutions and workouts benefit all parties.

In Canada, unlike the United States, the concept of a "pre-packaged 11" is not known. In the prepackaged, everything is negotiated and resolved in advance and the court is presented with a fait accompli for its approval. The costs are low and the timing is immediate, with maximum preservation of value.

This key direction must be developed and followed in Canada if management and shareholders are truly interested in preserving businesses. Creditors and lawyers might be well advised to learn this methodology.

WHY ARE MOST REORGANIZATION PLANS UNSUCCESSFUL?

Most reorganizations under CCAA are unsuccessful and are eventually liquidated or become bankruptcies and are then liquidated. There are many reasons why a reorganization fails, and we don't always know the exact causes, but from the histories of debtors whose filings failed, some more common reasons are:

- Bad faith or naive optimism by the debtor in proposing a plan of reorganization based on revenue forecasts that were too optimistic and cost reductions that could not be effected;
- Changes in the economic climate that are beyond the control of the debtor (e.g., increases in interest rates driving down sales of new homes, forcing builders to fail; fare-wars cutting expected revenues of airlines; and the fall of the Canadian dollar);
- Management's failure to agree upon and to implement the staff and cost reductions needed for a company to survive;
- The uncovering, after application, of financial information that reveals the condition of the debtor to be much worse than was originally stated;
- The inability to obtain agreement of all classes of creditors to a plan of reorganization;
- The high fees paid to professionals in reorganizations may also contribute to the failure of the plan.

WHO SHOULD ADVISE YOU IN BANKRUPTCY?

Remember Polonius's advice to his son Laertes and take your own counsel first. Simply because your business has entered a troubled period is no reason to lose confidence in your leadership or business management abilities. You've probably already made the worst mistakes and you are on an uphill journey. The bankruptcy filing may provide the "fresh start" on your climb to the mountaintop and a successful business recovery. You will probably need legal bankruptcy counsel, but don't let the lawyer run wild and try to control your life. Use a bankruptcy lawyer for legal counsel and representation and not for any other purpose.

The Bankruptcy Lawyer's Role

The role of a bankruptcy lawyer, their business mission, is to represent your interests before the Commercial Court and to provide the company with legal counsel about the issues of creditors and bankruptcy.

> "Well, I don't know as I want a lawyer to tell me what I cannot do. I hire him to tell me how to do what I want to do."
> *J.P. Morgan (1837-1913)*

When Not to Listen to Your Lawyer

Bankruptcy lawyers usually have a stronger knowledge of accounting and business than other members of the bar, mostly because of the nature of the role they take in proceedings. They often act as if they were experts in business, but debtors must be wary of taking their business advice.

Most lawyers have no prior business experience other than working as an attorney, and unless they are a partner in their law firm, they usually have never even been responsible for a weekly payroll. Bankruptcy lawyers may be experienced at the management of bankruptcy cases, but they are rarely qualified to be business advisors or management consultants.

You wouldn't give much credibility to your dentist's advice on executing a new will, and you should not be giving credence to your lawyer's advice on matters that go beyond the legal scope of the bankruptcy filing.

We have asked many bankruptcy lawyers the following question: "If you were asked by a client to give business advice, would you?" All of the lawyers answered that they never give business advice, saying they were not qualified. Several told me although they had some business experience, they were lawyers not businesspersons.

The answers were what we expected, but anyone who has experience with bankruptcy lawyers would agree that these professionals cross the line and give business recommendations quite willingly.

Unfortunately many debtors, even those with decades of business experience, because of their predicament and feelings of helplessness, also misplace confidence in their lawyer's business counsel.

But don't place the blame upon your lawyer. Would you blame your dentist for giving you poor advice on estate planning? It's your own fault for listening to the advice.

> The failure of lawyers to limit their counsel to the practice of law is usually the result of the client's willingness to listen.

Meeting with a Bankruptcy Lawyer

Unless you are facing an imminent problem with a creditor that will impair your ability to conduct business, prepare carefully for your first meeting with a bankruptcy lawyer and assemble the documents listed.

DOCUMENTS TO PREPARE BEFORE MEETING A BANKRUPTCY LAWYER

1. List of all business liabilities, i.e., debts (include all accounts payable and all scheduled debts such as loans, mortgages, leases, credit card payments, and utilities);

2. List of all business assets (include all bank accounts, stocks and investments, real estate, vehicles, major equipment, insurance claims due, accounts receivable, deposits, and refunds due);

   (Initially for items #1 and #2, to make a filing the lawyer will only need the name of the asset, debtor, or creditor and the amount or value. eventually the court will require the full name and address of each item on the lists.)

3. All of the obligations that you or other officers, managers, or employees, share or cosigned for on behalf of the business;

4. Details of any outstanding litigation or pending arbitration;

5. Copies of leases, contracts, loan documents, guarantees, and all security agreements;

6. Copies of tax claims and accounts owed;

7. Lists of any recently "bounced" cheques;

8. All cheques written and delivered or mailed to the payee, but not yet cleared the bank (include payroll and commission cheques);

9. If you, or other principals of the business are contemplating a personal bankruptcy filing, you will need personal lists for the items in #1 through #8, above;

   WARNING Consult with your personal lawyer before showing any of your personal exhibits to the company's bankruptcy counsel.

10. List of all wages, salaries, and commissions, past due;

11. List of any overdue taxes, particularly any "withholding" taxes (payroll taxes, health taxes, CPP, UIC, and workers' compensation.

These documents will make the meeting significantly more effective and should allow the lawyer to give you an analysis of your options and a better estimate of the costs involved.

Choosing a Lawyer

Shop around! Choosing a bankruptcy lawyer is no different than choosing a doctor for your children. You are placing a large part of your financial and business life in the lawyer's hands.

Discuss your case with at least two bankruptcy lawyers before making any decisions. If the lawyer, or their law firm, represents any of your creditors, they may be prohibited by a possible conflict of interest from representing you.

WARNING

To make the process of selecting a lawyer efficient, the first step should be to show the lawyer the debtor's **complete** list of creditors and potential claimants and ask them if they have any conflicts of interest **before** discussing the merits and the details of the case.

The fees for filing bankruptcy are similar throughout Canada, but this does not apply to the fees you will pay your bankruptcy lawyer for legal representation both prior to and during the pendency of the bankruptcy proceeding. All legal fees are negotiable and if you are not satisfied with the estimate, then continue shopping.

PREPARING FOR A POSSIBLE BANKRUPTCY FILING

Always consult at least one bankruptcy lawyer and consider seeking a second opinion before you decide how and when to file for bankruptcy.

When should you time your bankruptcy filing? The advice on when to file a bankruptcy is similar to the answer given to the new restauranteur when asking for advice on what three factors will make a restaurant successful. The answer is location, location, and location. When should you file for bankruptcy, when you have planned, planned, and planned.

A poorly timed filing is one done after the company has been padlocked by the bank, or evicted from its offices by the landlord, or its bank accounts seized by a judgement creditor. A filing done after any of these actions can still be useful, but doing it the week before would have been better timing.

If you owe most of your bills at the beginning of each month, don't pay all of your bills during the first week of the month and then file in the second week. Refrain from paying bills and stall creditors until the last possible date. When you have maximized the cash in your coffers, then you are ready to file. You will need money in the bank to survive a bankruptcy, and the only way you can accumulate it is not to pay creditors.

Funds Required

Work closely with your accounting staff and bankruptcy professionals to estimate the costs, including professional retainers of the first 90 days in bankruptcy. If you cannot build up a war chest of cash sufficient to last the first 60 to 90 days in bankruptcy, then you probably won't make it successfully through a CCAA.

CHAPTER 15

SOME FINAL THOUGHTS

REVERSE THE MANAGEMENT PROCESS FOR LONG-TERM SUCCESS

As the North American economy shows new signs of life and rebirth there will be the ever present threat of returning to the glorious days of "growth for its own sake" management styles of the 1980s. The sharp improvements in profitability, productivity, and competitiveness show that management is capable of "more and better" with less in the 1990s. The "virtual" or hollow organizations operating with 75% of their previous management force will remain meaningful for years to come. This is especially true in an economy based on competitiveness, being a low cost producer or retailer, and leading through innovation.

The process of economic and managerial transformation of the early 1990s has shown us that most of the concepts we espoused in the 1970s and 1980s about human resources were not efficient or effective. Excess perks and rewards produced a management that became lazy and unmotivated. The human resources dominance of the management process over leadership strategy and common sense produced bloated bureaucracies that were antientrepreneurial and incapable of managing change.

Everyone had a title. Secretaries became administrative assistants and everyone else was a coordinator, a term commonplace in the stagnant bureaucracy. But no one seemed responsible for getting things done.

Management guru Peter Drucker writes about the need to ensure that "responsibility should always exceed authority." This forces management to take risks, to innovate, and to force constant organizational changes.

We once found a government bureaucrat whose job title was "coordinating coordinator of coordination." He was responsible for ensuring that the meaningless process meetings held by department coordinators were scheduled properly and created meetings to ensure more meaningless meetings took place.

Reversing the management process forces us back to the basics. No rigid hierarchies, no meaningless titles, no unproductive incentives, bonuses, and benefits. The approach takes a realistic view of the world, making us a cash-conscious efficient team of change agents and ensuring the constant evolution of the business. Everything is questioned; our systems, our marketing, our compensation, our overhead. Those running the business must learn to think of the firm as being back at its entrepreneurial roots: lean, mean, efficient, and market-responsive.

There is no longer room out there for perks at 33% of salaries, golden parachutes, and first-class travel. We can no longer afford $60 a square foot for offices having 27 vice presidents with few responsibilities.

We spent 20 years convincing people they would succeed if they replicated the processes of "Big Business." That was entirely wrong. Big business can succeed only if each retail store in the system is an entrepreneurial and profitable unit and each service centre is a profit centre. A factory can survive in today's global markets only if it leads in productivity, is a low-cost producer, or leads in innovation.

Constantly reversing the process back to the entrepreneurial mode is what is needed. That mode is the most effective, and it is market-responsive. Nonperformers are fired; the perk is you get to keep your job. The success is that the business pays its bills and your salary. Its consumers determine almost every month if you deserve to live or die.

This is the stark reality of winning in the 1990s. It is about leadership: dealing with the problems and challenges of change and avoiding the turnaround process — forced change from without.

RECOMMENDED READING

A REVIEW OF BUSINESS TITLES in local bookstores has revealed few books currently available for the average business reader that teach the skills necessary for managing a turnaround.

The following are practical books that should prove useful to the manager of a troubled company already engaged in or contemplating a turnaround. The ordering of the titles is alphabetical and infers no ranking or preference.

Operational and Financial Turnarounds

Each of the following books was written by a principal or senior executive of a company that weathered the storm of business failure; the authors either succeeded in turning their company around or learned the lessons and succeeded with their next company. Although covering common territory, each author has a different approach to managing a turnaround.

Goldhammer, John. *The Save Your Business Book: A Survival Manual for Small Business Owners.* New York: Lexington Books, 1993, 235 pages.

Silver, David A. *The Turnaround Survival Guide: Strategies for the company in crisis.* Chicago: Dearborn Financial Publishing, Inc., 1992, 339 pages,

Tomasko, Robert M. *Downsizing: Reshaping the Corporation for the Future*. New York: American Management Association, 1987, paperback 1989, 290 pages.

Whitney, John O. *Taking Charge: How to Turn a Troubled Company Around — Straight to the Top*. New York: Warner Books, 1987, paperback 1992, 283 pages.

Marketing Turnarounds

Goldston, Mark R. *The Turnaround Prescription: Repositioning Troubled Companies*. New York: Free Press, 1992, 198 pages.

This book is different from the preceding titles because it is primarily concerned with managing a turnaround from a marketing viewpoint. Once your company has stabilized its financial base, the next step is not only to recover lost marketing territory but to gain the commanding heights. It would be worthwhile to read this book prior to planning the resurrection of your business.

INDEX